FAY

ANGUS

The Catalyst

Tyndale House
Publishers, Inc.
Wheaton, Illinois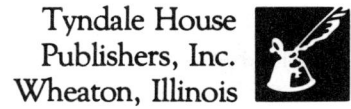

Quotes in Chapter 7 are
from *The Saving Life of
Christ*, W. I. Thomas,
© 1961 by Zondervan
Publishing House. Used
by permission.

NOTE: In order to
protect the privacy of
many people mentioned
in this book, the names
have been changed.

First printing, November
1979. Printed in the
United States of
America.

For John,

husband and friend

CONTENTS

ONE
ALBERNI STREET

ALBERNI STREET was drenched! Torrents of rain were steadily turning the weekend snowfall into puddles of muddy slush. Arm in arm, clutching a soggy brown paper bag of groceries and sharing a single umbrella, Mother and I bent head-on into the wind and struggled forward.

"Now try to remember, Bubs, which house did you see her come out of?" Mother's voice was irritable as we paused.

"Oh, dearly beloved St. Anthony," I prayed, "finder of lost objects, surely you're a finder of lost persons, too. . . . Please find her for us!" Drat it! Why hadn't I paid more attention when I saw her?

We had stopped at two houses already. "Yes," they knew the old woman, "No," they didn't know where she lived, and what did we want with her, anyway? Everyone laughed at her and she was said to be quite mad. Eccentric, maybe, I thought, but not mad; no, never mad.

She drifted through the seasons, a humped-over figure shuffling along in slippers, sagging socks, and shabby coat. She spent her meager funds on scraps of fish for the groups of stray cats that rubbed and purred around her ankles. They seemed to come from nowhere when they saw her, trailing litters of half-starved kittens, scurrying out from under houses and up and down the alleys.

I spoke to her one day—turning abruptly, she had fixed me with a stare that startled me. Her eyes were blue. This was a shock. I had expected gray, or green, or tawny amber, dulled with vacancy . . . but blue? A piercing blue? Mesmerized, I walked on.

Slowly through the weeks she gave recognition to my flying figure as I raced to and from the local ballet studio clad in long black tights. She gave a slight nod of the head, or her body twisted around to watch me running down the street. Perhaps she saw a panther in my stride, a wild jungle cat, a kinship to her own lost brood. Captive in the asylums of her own deep griefs, she never smiled, but slowly, in her own peculiar way, she drew me to her.

One day she spoke. It whips my memory . . . a quiet, cultured tone. "What is your name?" Her eyes were full of tears. Our hands reached out to clasp and friendship grew between lithesome, hurried girl and tattered, aging soul.

In her I saw the sorrows of the centuries; she had her counterpart in every age, trembling, clinging to the fringe of life itself. Within the cloister of her mind, her plodding dedication to her cats reflected a strange nobility. The only love she had to give was lavished on a huge black cat named Tom. One day he struggled to her, convulsed, and died within her arms. It broke her already sagging heart. Poisoned? But why? She never was the same. Tears continually filled the creases on her face and she'd wander up and down the street calling to him, "Tom, come, Tom . . . Tom. . . ."

We hadn't seen her for weeks. Alberni cats were hungry.

Timidly we knocked at yet another house. A disheveled man came to the door. "Yeah . . . down the hall, on the right."

The stench of stale fish assaulted us. Coughing violently, we entered the tiny room. We had found her. Blending into the rags that covered the bed, she was practically indistinguishable save for a few lumpy contours and the movement of her rapid breathing.

We choked in our near-nausea and showed her the bottles of homemade soup and jello that we had brought.

"Beef tea," my mother said; "that'll build you up!"

She could barely lift her head. Beads of sweat matted the hair across her brow and she looked up at us with fogged eyes. Damp laundry hung from ceiling strings, and on the double gas hot plate a pot of giblets simmered, steaming up the single window that was shut tight against the battering rain. On its narrow ledge purred a huge calico, paws neatly tucked under her massive hulk. She blinked her yellow eyes at me.

We had moved to Alberni Street in the spring and obtained a fairly decent suite of rooms with a closet kitchen on a top floor. It was in one of the many rooming houses that stretched through Vancouver's West End, all the way from the courthouse to the gates of its famed Stanley Park. We were close to the shops, the Canadian National Telegraph Office where I had a job as a junior clerk, the beaches of English Bay, and best of all, the ballet studio where I tried to dance and dance and dance away the memories of war.

The night shadows were still there—moments when I would awaken and instinctively reach out for the mosquito net that had tucked me into my prison cot, or sleep with my head entirely covered by the bedclothes to avoid the glare of the guard's spot-check torch.

China was a half a world away, yet always an eternal present infused into my very life blood—a pulse of memory. The experiences of concentration camp had been stamped across my inner being as though they were tattooed across my body.

Indeed, the Japanese invasion of Shanghai, with all its appendant hardships of incarceration, had reduced the joyous experiences of my childhood into short, scattered memories. They were memories to which I clung with zealous tenacity and rehearsed constantly in my mind, lest they be obliterated by the psychological impact of war. I had been a stubborn, determined child; I was emerging into a stubborn, determined woman—determined to pick up the threads of my life, come what may, determined not to be crippled by the past ordeal, and determined to proceed with vigor. I had survived, I was very much alive, I was seventeen!

We had crossed the Pacific in a freighter—twelve passengers, four to a cabin. The promise of a new life in a new world had built dreams in every white-capped wave. I spent endless hours pacing the decks, looking up at cloud patterns in the sky and then down at foam patterns in the sea. Caught between, man walks and walks and walks, I thought. I saw the hand of a mighty Creator in both, and I learned there were times to look up and times to look down. I resolved that no matter to what heights of good fortune or depths of despair I traveled, I would look beyond—to the Hand that traced the pattern. It was a Hand that had wrapped itself around my life during the rigors of our imprisonment; it was a Hand in which I had put my trust; it was a Hand to which I clung; it held my security, my hope, my comfort, my strength, and my destiny.

We were at sea when the first underwater atomic bomb was tested. Our ship had instructions to divert course and to observe and report. It was a time of anticipation. The crew was on full alert. Unfortunately, being so far out of range of the test site, we saw and felt only a growing swell of the ocean. We sailed into the tail end of a typhoon—a glorious time of whistling high winds and raging waves that tossed and pitched us like a bobbing cork! All the passengers got sick except me! The hatches were battened down and everyone had strict instructions to stay below. As the ship would roll, all one could see out of the portholes were the wrestling waves. The dishes on the dinner tables slid from side to side, clattering into the restraining rails placed on tables.

It was exhilarating. I loved every moment of the storm and had grand fun trying to keep my balance; legs astride, arms outstretched, I bent with the rolls and laughed at the frailty of men when pitted against the powers of the universe! Like Job, I saw the "whirlpools of the deep . . ." and knew that "the Spirit of God hath made me, and the breath of the Almighty hath given me life. . . ."

As we sailed through the beautiful Straits of Georgia and slid under the famed Lions Gate Bridge, my heart raced. The dawn of that new life! An arrival from the Orient was news; reporters met us as we berthed and I answered their questions shyly, my eyes scanning the dock, wondering which of all the people clustered there would be our relatives. I saw no children, yet I knew I had two cousins with my aunt and uncle. The plan was for Mother to leave me in their care. Then after we had a brief holiday and rest together, she would return to her position in Shanghai with Butterfield and Swire, the large shipping firm. I would attend the University of British Columbia and pursue the teaching career upon which I had built so many dreams.

My uncle was alone. We fell into his arms. Soon he was piling our suitcases into his car. As we drove through the wonderland of Stanley Park, awed by the towering Canadian Douglas firs—over the very same bridge I had watched rise out of the early morning mists—I caught the words "tensions, divorce, I'm so sorry. . . ." "You should have written . . . we would never have come . . . what can we do?"

We had walked into a hornet's nest. The home that we had expected to welcome us for a few months of rehabilitation and adjustment, the family that was to have housed and guided me through my years of study, was in the midst of emotional trauma. It was being quickly ripped apart.

We moved as soon as we could.

Alberni was a side street, off the beaten path even of foot traffic. It gave no diplomas, but offered credentials no school could match! It was the introduction to a fringe society that cut deep insights into me. We walked a lot, my mother and I. Her health was still gravely impaired from the years of internment, and it was good for her to take the air, strolling slowly to the park. She would sit for hours in healing serenity and feed the ducks that quacked their way 'round and 'round the willow trees of Lost Lagoon.

It was on these walks that we met the struggle on Alberni. The cat woman mucking her way about, distributing her bits of fish; then two sisters, tiny wizened figures, huddled together in black fur-trimmed overcoats. Their heads were generally bent to hide the scar tissue that stretched taut across their heavily powdered faces. They looked like painted marionettes, with deep-sunken eyes peering out of papier-mâché masks. Victims of a fire, they had spent the past ten years in secluded loneliness, locked only to each other.

"At least they have each other," my mother said, "the same as we have each other."

"Yes," I agreed, but what would happen, I wondered, when one of them died? Their faces were stretched beyond any lines or expression and only wisps of graying hair peeking out from under their broad-brimmed hats gave any indication whatsoever of how old they might be.

The day-in-day-out monotony of their lonely lives and their inevitable future bereavement kept me aware that there was suffering and anguish in this brand new world. This reality was not like the abandoned babies of China, or the corpses strewn about the streets of Shanghai during cholera season. Not like the beggars crying from gutters, nor like the gnawing hunger of concentration camp, or the piercing screams of the torture chambers.

To see it you had to walk with it, to live with it, to reach out and touch it. It was the filter holding back the sun in darkened lives. It was heart's sorrow: abrasive, buried both in affluence and poverty. It was the beginning of an understanding that was later to let me penetrate and weep through the heartaches of the drug culture in America.

Another character in our life, the professor of Alberni Street, was elegantly frayed. I studied him with delightful curiosity and took great amusement and pleasure in his jaunty arrogance. Tall and lean, he was never without a flower in his buttonhole—rosebud, pansy, buttercup, or even dandelion, depending on the season and the route he took on his walk. He swung a cane and generally whistled his way though trouble. His tattered tweed overcoat with its faded velvet collar, spats on his shoes, woolen gloves, and huge muffler made one think of Charles Dickens' A *Christmas Carol*! His theatrical airs fit him ideally into the story, but I could never quite make up my mind whether he should be Bob Cratchit or Scrooge!

A shock of white hair, his unshaven chin, and wild, wandering eyes belied the sharpness of his mind and wit. He carried a briefcase full of musical scores and old newspaper clippings, mostly about himself and his concert performances. He was quick to boast the distinction of having once met the Prince of Wales. He loved the arts passionately and was a regular visitor to the ballet studio, much to the dismay of Madame. On hearing the tap of his cane on the stairs, she would shut her eyes, clutch her forehead in mock alarm, and groan, "No, I cannot stand it today. I cannot stand it!" Then she'd laugh, and we'd all laugh, and he'd walk in.

He would lean against the piano, tap time to the music with his cane, and direct a constant commentary to Madame on the virtues or faults of this or that student while she pretended not to notice him. Occasionally the dancers would curtsy and bow to him with exaggerated respect, winking mischievously at each other. Nothing escaped him. He'd jut his chin forward and squint at them, finally giving them a good poke with his cane.

When his visit was over he'd bend, shower dandruff all over Madame, and kiss her loudly on the cheek.

"The germs . . ." she'd wail after he'd gone, "that terrible man . . ." Then she'd fly off to the bathroom for a good scrub.

There was a time when I, too, thought "that terrible man," and wished I didn't know him. At concerts, plays, or the ballet, after the first intermission, the ushers would frequently let the professor in to some unoccupied seat in the balcony. One might say he had a free season's pass to the latter half of every theatrical attraction in town.

Settling into the second act of *Giselle* one night, he slipped into the seat behind me. Recognition was inevitable.

"Fay, what a pleasure. How are you?" The resonance of his voice must have carried well down into the orchestra pit.

I froze and whispered through a weak smile, "Thank you, I'm fine."

"Speak up, speak up, eh . . . what's that?"

"I'm fine, thank you, fine. . . . Shh-h, the music's starting!"

"Good, now tell me, how's Lois dancing tonight?"

By now eyes were turning up to the balcony to view this odd tattered man and small elfin girl shouting genialities to each other.

"Fay, look at that; David has improved. . . . Bravo, bravo!"

I left before the final curtain—I didn't want to be recognized as the one in the shouting match! But the professor was right, David had improved—David and Lois, Sonia, Marguerite, and the many students from the studio who had graduated to the professional stage with the National Ballet Company of Canada.

After such performances I would spend days imagining myself in the leading roles of all the ballets in the repertoire and I'd do all my filing at the telegraph office on demi-point or with one foot tucked neatly into the *cou-de-pied* (neck-of-the-foot—ankle) of the other. Anything to strengthen my balance and technique.

Alberni Street delivered to us our own personal struggle. A letter from Taikoo. It came just over a year after the post-war communiqué from head office.

Taikoo—the Chinese name given to the Blue Funnel Line, Butterfield & Swire, shipping giant of the China/India trade. The word meant "honorable, great, old, enduring."

The October '45 communiqué had first remembered those on staff who had given their lives for King and Country: sixty-seven of them who went to war at sea, on land, or in the air, and perished at the hands of the enemy.

The London staff has carried on with complete calm and regularity despite bombs, fires, damage, or destruction of their homes. . . .

The men in the ships in the face of the peril of the war at sea have maintained the reputation of the Taikoo fleet and have as usual done their duty despite strange and bad crews, difficulties in victualling and repairs, Government control, and in too many cases anxiety about the fate of their nearest and dearest interned in the hands of the enemy. . . .

The calmness and nerve of those who had to remain at their posts in China and Hong Kong, knowing the nigh certainty of privation, ill-treatment, humiliation, and perhaps torture at the hands of the enemy. . .

When release came, those who, forgetful of their personal wishes to see their homes and enjoy some let-up, did not wait for help, but set to work themselves on reconstruction, even before the flag fell, and British trade as well as Taikoo must be grateful to them. . . ."

Then, the very essence of the directive of the letter:

There are still many and great dangers to be overcome before we reach the open sea, and we shall need all our courage and initiative and powers of work and (perhaps more than all) patient staying power. None the less, with these examples during the past war years before us, we do not fear for the future of Taikoo and we know that its prestige was never higher as a good servant of England and China. And the spirit of service is what really matters in the world. The directors would like to wish you all good luck and to express their pride at being fellow servants with all of you of a firm engaged in the great adventure of the China trade which Mr. J.S. Swire called the Blue Riband of Trade. . . .

"Courage, initiative, and patient staying power" were not enough. A rebel called Mao Tse-tung was grinding his Communist forces against the Chinese mainland. Foreign investment and the "great adventure of the China trade," which began in 1275 when Marco Polo arrived in Peking at the invitation of Kublai Khan, had come to an end. China was soon to belong once again only to the Chinese people. The bamboo curtain was rapidly falling.

The Alberni Street letter said, "Do not return, danger is imminent." My mother's hand trembled as she put it down. There was nothing to say. China was her roots, her job, her security, her happiness, her life. She had left two generations of memories in its soil, and one small son buried under a white marble slab, given back to the Chinese earth. Her world was no more.

For me it meant the end of my dreams of college; it meant the end of any thoughts of a ballet career; it meant a bread-and-butter discipline in the serious business of earning our living.

Rain clouds hung over Sleeping Beauty Ridge and the twin lion peaks from which the bridge got its name. Hands in pockets, head down, I went out into the drizzle and kicked a pebble all the way down Alberni to the Lost Lagoon of the park. "Don't let go of us, God," I whispered. "Please, don't let go!"

TWO
THE MISCHIEF-MAKERS

JUST WHO taught my father, I don't know, but my father taught my mother and my mother taught me. It was not difficult to contact spirits, especially if one had the sixth (psychic) sense that tuned in phenomena beyond normal dimensions.

In his *Screwtape Letters*, C.S. Lewis has said; "There are two equal and opposite errors into which our race can fall about the devils. One is to disbelieve their existence. The other is to believe and to feel an excessive and unhealthy interest in them."

I had grown up in an environment that accepted the spirit world as part of daily life. Paul wrote, "for we wrestle not against flesh and blood, but against principalities, against powers, against the rulers of the darkness of this world, against spiritual wickedness in high places. . . ."

The Chinese had a great respect and fear for those "rulers of the darkness of this world." They went to great lengths to appease or to avoid them. They consulted the oracles concerning every aspect of their lives. The local fortune-teller was a prominent, important member of the community and did a thriving business, often serving as a *controlling spirit* in the lives of his clientele. He advised the day on which to be married, the omens for good business, the place in which to be buried. Fortune-tellers burned their joss incense sticks to ward off evil spirits. Even Chinese architecture reflected belief in spirits; roofs were designed with corners curved upward so that demons sliding down could not get into the building but would be shot skyward again.

Demon gods were greatly feared. Indeed, a boy child was so highly valued in Chinese culture that his parents would frequently give him a girl's name and put earrings on him to deceive the spirits. It was also said that devils could not turn corners, so screens were put in doorways and zigzag walks and bridges built to confuse them. If adversity came to a man, it was probably because a demon was following him, and men often darted frantically in front of trams, automobiles, or buses so that an evil spirit on their trail would be killed in that fraction of an instant after they themselves barely escaped. Unfortunately, many misjudged that fraction of an instant and died in tragic, futile attempts at deliverance.

I had grown up accustomed to the clicking fortune sticks of the Chinese soothsayer—generally a blind man led through the city streets by a child. We would invite him in to entertain at parties. For a few coppers he would conjure up a future of adventures and dramatically stun his audience with the accuracy of his insight into the past and present lives of those around the room.

I remember quaking at the knees when one such blind man looked straight at me with his sightless eyes and rattled off a long string of predictions about me to my mother. She smiled, so they must have been good, and I'm sure he was aware that a good fortune always brought in an extra coin or two. I studied the little girl who led him around; she couldn't have been more than six or seven, and I wondered what it would be like to walk with and learn from such a seemingly supernatural being. I was awed and scared and quite fascinated.

My various amahs had taught me much about Chinese symbolism. They saw spirits everywhere. The earliest records of their religion said that out of a "nebulous, bubbling chaos" came Yang, the active masculine light of the universe, and Yin, the passive, dark feminine principle. From the union of Yang and Yin a dwarf named P'an Ku was born and he spent eighteen thousand years building the universe. He grew and grew as he was building and when he finally died his head became the mountains, his breath the mists, clouds, and winds; his eyes the sun and moon; his veins the rivers; his teeth and bones the minerals.

My eyes would grow wide with wonder as I listened to all these stories, and when the cold wind blew I knew that P'an Ku must be getting very angry. One of his eyes blinked at me from the sun by day, and the other shone through the shadows of my curtained windows by night.

One of my amahs was addicted to the theater and frequently, when she was supposed to be taking me down to the park for a walk, we would end up instead watching a series of fascinating, colorful dramas. These were mythical plays complete with actors in ferocious masks. Every emotion was acted out with exaggerated gestures to the beat of drums, cymbals, and the famous two-stringed fiddle.

That particular amah taught me about the swallows who, when they fly into a home, bring prosperity and success. About the plum blossoms (courage and hope), chrysanthemums (the last flower to bloom before winter, symbolizing longevity), geese (happy married life, because they take only one mate). About fish, tigers, horses, and all the other symbols that color their way through Chinese art and mythology.

As a result it has always been a bit difficult for me to acknowledge the dragon of our Western culture as the embodiment of Satan or a demon or hell, because in the Chinese culture the dragon is the most supreme of all symbolic beasts and stands for goodness, strength, and benevolence. Why on earth would St. George have wanted to slay him?

Epilepsy was generally interpreted as spirit possession, especially in Kansu and Yunnan provinces, which were greatly influenced by the monasteries of Tibet. Demon dancers in grotesque masks and glittering costumes twirled their way through festivals while everyone anxiously awaited the appearance and trance of the Sung-ma. Sung-mas of the Tibetan lamaseries are the demon-possessed oracles of the faith, abodes of malignant spirits, and they play an important role in the selection of the Dalai Lama.

These are men given to epileptic seizures, and during the trance or seizure they are said to be the mouthpiece of the powerful spirit indwelling them. Any man who has such seizures is generally highly regarded and elevated to the honored priesthood of Sung-ma.

Is it any wonder that Mao Tse-tung in his red sweep of China abolished all religion? The Chinese people were a society crippled by religious superstition; the tragedy is that Mao threw out the liberating truth of the gospel of Jesus Christ in the process.

I had read tea leaves and told fortunes with playing cards ever since I could remember. It was part of the "game," and as I grew older it soon ceased to be a game and became an intense involvement—especially at the ballet studio where I was sought after for advice about love, money, career, and to satisfy a general mumbo-jumbo of curiosity.

"C'mon Fay," the students would say, "read our cards. . . ."

We'd pull out a deck, giggle, and I'd dramatically flip the shuffle and start laying out the individual destinies.

All this was about to spill over into a more deadly preoccupation—an opportunity to personally contact the spirit world.

My mother had cut letters of the alphabet out of the cardboard backing that came with packages of nylon stockings. These were placed in a circle on top of our small round coffee table, with an empty tumbler of light glass turned over in the center. We had invited Mrs. Graham, from the rooms next door, to participate in the séance. Rosemary Graham was a tiny Englishwoman with transparent skin and a puckish quality that bubbled over in good humor. She worked as a clerk in the famous Hudson's Bay Company and rushed home each day utterly exhausted, slipped into a comfortable pair of beige moccasins and a chenille robe, and flopped down for a cup of tea with Mother.

They soon became good friends. I don't know where her husband was—whether they had drifted apart or divorced, or whether he had died was a question we never brought up. I do know she had a delightful son who had married a girl who was a "complete twit," according to Mrs. Graham, and it was all a dreadful pity!

We drew the drapes against the twilight and took our places around the little table. Only two could contact at a time, so I had to watch as Mum and Mrs. G. each lightly placed the tips of the central finger of her right hand on the edge of the tumbler.

"Hardly touch it at all, Rose," my mother whispered. "Sometimes it'll even move when you're just above it."

I sat with my eyes glued to the empty overturned glass. It all seemed too simple, somehow. An eerie stillness fell over the room. It emphasized the loud thumping of my quickened heartbeat.

Suddenly there was a slight vibration of the glass.

"Yes?" said my mother. "Yes? Is somebody there?"

Slowly the glass moved around the letters and spelled out a quivery "Y-E-S."

I could hardly breathe!

"Who's there?" asked my mother. "Identify yourself, please."

"J-O-S-E-L-Y-N," spelled the glass.

My mother went ashen.

"J-O-S-E-L-Y-N W-H-I-T-E," the glass went on. "N-i-c-e t-o c-o-n-t-a-c-t y-o-u, A-m-y."

"A childhood friend," Mother whispered to us. "She was killed in an accident years ago."

"The spirits must identify themselves," my mother had cautioned us before we began. "You must know who you are talking to, otherwise it can become quite dangerous." I didn't dare to think of what she might mean by "dangerous," and I didn't ask.

I could hardly wait for my turn. My fingers barely skimmed the glass and it didn't even look as though Mother's were on it at all.

"F-A-Y, B-U-B-S-I-E F-A-Y," the glass spelled out.

"Who is it?" I asked. "Please identify yourself."

There was a long pause, then "J-U-L-I-E."

"Julie!" Best-beloved of all my childhood friends. Dearest confidante; closest intimate. After the war and rigors of internment she had developed tuberculosis and had been whisked away with her family to the Italian Alps to take the cure.

She had written regularly from her chaise longue, wrapped in muffling blankets, lying out amid the snow-covered mountains. Confident of her "cure," she had then gone down to Milan to enroll in University, studying in Italian for her degree in sociology. Despite her exposure to the malaise of China, the poverty of postwar Italy startled her. She wrote pitiful letters about men, women, and children living in the ruins of bombed-out buildings. To help, I'd beg my friends for their cast-off clothing. I managed to send her a few boxes of overcoats, sweaters, and other warm garments, which she delightfully distributed.

Then she'd get a relapse of the dreaded TB and be off for another rest in the Alps. Abruptly came that terrible silence.

I wrote and wrote everywhere, to every address she had ever given me. Silence. I wrote to her father's address; I wrote to her uncle's address; I wrote to England where she had spent a short vacation. Silence. I wondered if she were dead. It seemed the only possibility. We had vowed to write, always, no matter what, no matter how. Her last letter to me had ended "Cheerio, Darling, scribble me a note soon as I get lonely for your letters."

If ever there was a way for me to be ensnared into the world of spiritism it would be through Julie. I could never resist the call of her name or of her voice. What I did not know at that time was that we were dabbling with what the Bible calls *familiar spirits*. It was a spirit disguised in the identity of a human being and masquerading as that human being, dead or alive.

These were not Julie, or Joselyn White, or anyone else who spoke under a name we knew. These were familiar spirits, ensnaring spirits, using our emotional involvement with the dead to snag us.

This was the beginning of what I was later to find the Bible called an "abomination unto the Lord" (Deut. 18). We did not know the Scriptures, so we were easily ensnared and soon became addicted to spiritism.

At the name "J-U-L-I-E" my eyes filled with tears. This could only mean for sure that she was dead. Great shaking sobs wracked my body.

From that day forward we contacted the spirits several times a week. My vivid imagination pictured them hovering about the room and I wondered what they looked like in their ethereal state. I would talk endlessly to Julie through the overturned glass; many other spirits came in and out of our séances.

I was working during the day at my job with the telegraph office; I was dancing at ballet classes and rehearsals late, until all hours of the evening; and every moment of my spare time was spent with the drapes drawn, with Rose and Mother, and the round table full of letters. I became thin, pale and wan. I'd awake in the morning feeling as though I had an acute case of pleurisy; my muscles ached from head to toe from all the strenuous ballet exercises; I developed a persistent cough.

We had many laughs. Rose was contacting one day when suddenly the spirit said "W-h-a-t's h-a-p-p-e-n-i-n-g t-o P-a-c-i-f-i-c P-e-t-e, R-o-s-e?" Rose nearly fell off her chair—Pacific Petroleum Corporation, the stock that both she and Mother had invested some dribs of money in, was slowly rising, and around it they built great hopes of grand profits.

"Yes? Yes?" replied Rose. "What do you know about Pacific Pete? Is it going up?"

"N-o," replied the glass, "s-e-l-l."

Rose and Mum looked at each other. This was something new; was the spirit world going to start advising them in the stock market? They were hesitant to sell their pet, and they missed the boat. It tumbled within a few days and it was too late to take their profit.

Both Rose and Mother had a lot of fun "talking stock market" with the spirits. Neither had much money to invest and their main interest was a quick turnover and a few dollars' profit.

As Mother and I were contacting one day, the glass suddenly spun about and twirled right out of our fingertips! Puzzled, we resumed our position. It then rushed around and around the letters nonstop—we could hardly keep up with it. During all our previous sessions the glass had moved very slowly. It was a rather long, drawn-out affair to carry on a conversation; we could verbalize our own questions and dialogue, but then had to patiently wait for the spirits to spell out the letters in each word of their answers.

This rushing glass was something different.

"Yes? Yes?" Mother asked. "Who's there?"

"T-E-D," spelled the glass.

"Ted?" we queried; we didn't know any Ted.

"H-A, H-A," went the glass; then, very rapidly, "H-a-a, h-a, h-a!" Once again it spun out of our control.

Suddenly I remembered the Ted of my father's war experience. I didn't know him, but my father had sent me a beautiful poem on his death in the battle of Repulse Bay, Hong Kong.

Ted! They said that you were dead—
I stooped and looked into your eyes
Wide-open, gazing far beyond the bounds
of all senescent flesh.
They held no vestige of surprise
Only dark implacable reflection.

High upon your forehead
the clotted stain of death's red touch
Scarce mars a face so rapt in dreams celestial,
and death's swift thrust was such
That it remains for you forever unsuspected. . . .

The poem went on and on in reflective verse. Was this that same Ted?

Actually it was not. It was a wandering spirit seeking embodiment in a human being, looking for an abiding place.

But believing that he might indeed be my father's friend and would perhaps talk about my dad, we chatted with him for a bit, and then asked him to go so that we could speak to someone else. On the command of "leave" the spirit had to leave. I don't know why. That was the instruction of my mother and somehow it worked. The human seemed to have complete control over the spirits—that is, until or unless a demonic spirit actually sought embodiment in a human being.

Ted changed the whole manner of our contacting. He was fast, rambunctious, sometimes hilariously funny with his remarks; and then as we proceeded, risqué, and eventually quite lewd.

In his book *I Talked with Spirits* (Tyndale), Victor Ernest says: "There are different kinds of spirits (Mark 9:29)—some are sensual and lewd and others appear ethical."

Ted started interrupting and interfering with all our other contacts, with those "ethical" spirits who were not at all offensive, quite congenial, and validated themselves by their knowledge of the friend they presumed to be or the private circumstances of our own lives. As we were engrossed talking to them, suddenly the glass would rush wildly about, and we'd have to say "All right, Ted, is that you again?"

He'd reply, quite demurely and slowly, "I-t's m-e a-l-l r-i-g-h-t. H-a, h-a, j-o-k-e!"

We'd tell him to leave, and he would for a few moments and then he'd be back again disrupting our séance.

Rose and I were contacting one day, talking to another spirit after having just dismissed Ted. My mother was sitting watching us from the couch when something suddenly shoved her and almost knocked her off. It happened again, and then again.

We asked the spirit we were contacting, "Was that Ted?"

"Y-e-s," replied the glass, "i-t w-a-s h-i-m, a-l-l r-i-g-h-t."

He started asking to talk to me all the time and wouldn't give us any peace until we agreed. "If we let you talk to Fay, will you then go away?"

"Y-e-s," he'd promise.

I'd come on and then he'd start flirting with me, making some remark about my pretty hair, body, or dancer's legs. He took on the role of suitor, wooing me. It became almost impossible to contact anyone else. Ted was always there. I wondered if he hovered about Alberni Street, just waiting for our contact glass to turn over.

After one particularly disruptive séance, he came and saucily asked "F-A-Y, w-i-l-l y-o-u m-a-r-r-y m-e?"

Rose, Mother, and I were horrified and frightened. At first we thought he was just being funny; then we realized that he was seeking to possess me—to be the controlling spirit of my life.

It was that final act that convinced my mother we must stop the contacting for a while anyway. I didn't quite understand what it all meant but I was curiously afraid. We stopped the contacting, but it was not the end of our occult involvement.

My mother had a friend from Shanghai who had "the gift." An attractive woman with large, deeply set eyes, she was a crystal gazer and professional astrologer. She claimed to be a Christian, saying she had been given this gift by God to help people. She even tithed 10 percent of all her earnings and sent the money to the Catholic fathers in Ireland. I doubt that the fathers had any idea where the money was coming from and it's just as well they didn't.

The fact was, she did help a lot of people.

I recall the especially memorable case of one of her clients. She had an office on the fourth floor of one of the large hotels in downtown Vancouver, and one day while entering the elevator she got "her vibrations" and turned to the gentleman on her left.

"You will not find your daughter in Vancouver," she said.

The man was completely taken aback. "Who are you?" he asked.

"I am a clairvoyant," Mrs. X replied, "and I know why you're here. If you like, you can come to my office and I will give you a crystal reading. I believe I can find your daughter for you."

She had never seen the man in her life. Indeed, he was an American businessman who had traveled to Vancouver for the express purpose of finding his daughter who had been missing for months.

He went for the reading.

"She is up the coastline." Looking deep into the crystal, Mrs. X continued, "I see her here in a town, it could be Prince Rupert. There are railroad tracks there, and she is in a small house."

The man was on the next train to Prince Rupert. He found his daughter in a small house close by the tracks. He returned and gave Mrs. X a check for 200 American dollars; 20 dollars of that went to the fathers in Ireland.

Mrs. X was constantly after us to let her give us readings. For some reason my mother held back, instinctively. She just did not want to get involved with the woman, and after what had happened with Ted and me, she did not want to endanger me.

Mother had always been very psychic. She heard things and saw things, besides doing excellent card-telling and accurate tea-leaf reading. I didn't mind the readings, but I was terrified that someday I, too, might "see" something. I just didn't like the idea of a visible ghost or spirit.

"Don't worry," Mother would say, "if something comes to visit you in the night, just tell it to come next door and see me."

"Oh, no," I thought. "Please, I don't want to see anything, ever!" I'd go to sleep with a trembling prayer, "Please, dear Lord, don't let anything come and visit me tonight!"

One morning my mother looked rather haggard. "Did you hear anything last night, Bubs?" she asked.

"No," I replied, wondering what was bothering her.

"Well, I certainly did. There were all sorts of bumps and it seemed as though the ornaments on the shelves were wobbling or rattling."

This went on for several weeks and broke Mother's sleep a great deal. We didn't know what it was. Then we found them. . . .

The rooming house was old, and above each doorway was a rather wide strip of molding with a slightly hollowed-out area. I was vacuuming there on a "once a month thorough cleaning" spree when the brush of the vacuum knocked off two strange little figures.

"What on earth are these?" I asked, taking them in to Mother.

"Where did you find them?" she said anxiously. I told her and her eyes grew dark in anger.

"These are 'mischief-makers.' They must be the reason for all the strange noises we've been hearing. Now I know . . . Mrs. X must be furious with us for not getting involved with her readings. The last time she was here she must have hidden them up there to make mischief in our lives!"

"Mischief-makers," I thought. . . . "What strange sort of power could two ugly little ceramic figures have?" Many years later in a canyon in California I was to find out.

THREE
DOBBS

DOBBS was in town, and that meant church twice on Sundays and probably a midweek prayer meeting. There was no choice, I either had to go with him or see him in between services. Rats!

We had met in concentration camp, two children of destiny thrown together by the Japanese invasion of China. "Dobbs," Derek Harrigan, son of missionary parents, with hair as red as the Irish blood that flowed through his veins, and eyes as blue as the heaven he preached. First love—bobbing Adam's apple, bowed legs, freckles and all! He had an unconditional commitment to his faith and constantly answered all my questioning doubts by pointing his skinny finger to some relevant passage of Scripture in the large black Bible he toted around.

"Because God says so, not me, but God," he always said. "Here, Fay, read it for yourself. It's right here!"

I would have loved to trip him up and shatter his assurance. I spent hours thinking up impossibilities to which he surely couldn't find answers, but he even managed to wiggle out of those questions by hanging his hat onto a verse in Deuteronomy that said, "The secret things belong unto the Lord our God: but those things which are revealed belong unto us and to our children for ever, that we may do all the words of this law" (29:29).

"If I didn't love him," I thought, "I'd probably hate him!"

But I did trip him up in other ways . . . I'd fling myself into his arms, and glue my body against his. I knew that he'd bend and melt when my arms were around him and my head was buried in the hollow of his neck. At times like that I had the upper hand. He'd kiss me passionately over and over again and I knew how desperately he wanted me.

Even though I wore the pretty little blue glass ring he had given me when we parted in Shanghai after the war, I was *second place* in his life. Second place to his God, second place to his Scriptures, and second place to what he constantly yapped about as "God's will."

That's what he was saying now: "If it's God's will, Fay, I'll come back and we'll be married."

We were wrapped together in a plaid lap blanket, cuddled against the chilly Vancouver night air, lying on a strip of sandy beach in between the huge boulders at English Bay, as the crashing waves and eerie moonlight played shadows on our bodies. Now and then errant bits of ocean spray stretched far enough to spatter our faces.

This was our favorite spot. We'd walk hand in hand or arm in arm around Stanley Park, sit for hours watching the seagulls squawk at each other, or practice skimming pebbles to see how many jumps they would make before sinking in the dark waters. Then we'd wrap up in the blanket, huddle together, and just be. How we ever managed to keep our purity under such close body contact, God alone knows, but we did. Biblical rules were biblical rules; Dobbs saw to it that we kept them.

I resented God's will in his life. I didn't want him to say "If . . . then . . ." I wanted him to say, "I love you, I don't want anyone else but you—whether God wills it or not!"

Somehow I was playing second fiddle to an omnipotent power I couldn't shake. I didn't like it at all.

Dobbs was leaving for Korea, drafted into the American army. He was not one to try to get out of doing anything that he thought he ought to do. He did not feel that his three rigorous years as a prisoner of war excused him from duty to his country.

"It's not fair," I whined. "You shouldn't have to go. We've just got together again."

Indeed, it wasn't fair. After serving as a POW he shouldn't *have* to go into the army, he shouldn't *want* to go into the army, and he should definitely *refuse* to go into the army! Where was "God's will" in this annoying situation? Besides, who would hold me in his strong arms, kiss my eyelids, and lie wrapped in a blanket with me on the sands of English Bay? There were other boys, yes, lots of them, interesting boys, fun boys, but they weren't Dobbs.

I had been going to the First Baptist Church in Vancouver's West End, within walking distance of our diggin's on Alberni Street. The Baptists were friendly, open people. They preached the necessity of a "born-again" experience with Jesus Christ, they baptized and, best of all, they had boys. Nice, born-again, baptized boys in various shapes and sizes. I was happy to attend their youth groups, participate in the frolic of their beach parties, and study their Scriptures.

Under the prayerful counseling of D. J. Watson—friend, father-confessor, spiritual teacher, missionary, and servant of the Lord, interned with us in the Yangchow prison camp—I had made a commitment to the Christian faith. That commitment was rapidly degenerating to one of convenience. Convenience to those things *I* chose to do, convenience to what *I* chose to think and what *I* chose to take priority in my life.

I dutifully read one chapter of the Bible each day, and found it terribly dull. I read it nevertheless, keeping my promise to D. J., skimming over the verses as quickly as I could so that I could say "That's that for today, God; thank you very much . . ." and go about the more important business of my social life, ballet, and general trivia of living.

Dobbs dragged me to all the evangelical churches in town, including his favorite "Tabernacle" where altar calls were given at each service. I could almost feel the pressure of his prayers at my side, "Get her forward, dear Lord!"

In turn, I'd drag him to our services at the Baptist Church where he'd boom out the hymns in a dominating voice that I'm sure had everyone looking at him. What his voice lacked in melodiousness it made up for in accuracy of note and volume. I'd cringe and shrink in embarrassment at his side, and resent his lack of vocal modesty and discretion.

I'd squirm my way through sermon after sermon, mentally blocking out the points that obviously hit home in my own spirituality, or lack of it, and restlessly look at my watch: "Ah, well, only seven more minutes of the service left to go, and that's it for another week!"

The fact of the matter was that the power of the Scriptures as preached by Dr. Paul from that evangelical pulpit was making me very uncomfortable. I had said yes to Christ, kneeling on the parched earth of the concentration camp; but I had not had the full "born-again" experience preached by the Baptists. That meant a new life, they said, with the indwelling presence of the Savior himself, working in and through the believer.

D. J. Watson wrote as often as he could. He had returned to his mission station in Hankow. Conditions there were hazardous as the Communists continued to sweep across China. Letters from him were a rare treat, and they bore stamps in denominations of 30,000 ridiculously devaluated Chinese dollars.

"Remember, Fay, commitment to Jesus is a moment-by moment, hour-by-hour act. . . . How I yearn for the day when my lassie gives herself entirely over to Christ . . . when she yields everything to him and he takes over all her thoughts, all her words, and all her actions. I pray for you daily."

At critical times of our lives almighty God in his merciful loving-kindness places within our vision his witnesses, his comforters, and his saints. The demonic spirit Ted was hovering over my shoulder due to my occult involvement, and although I had never made the contact with him again, I knew he was there, waiting to ensnare me. I had opened my life to the power of the "Prince of this world"; the very demons of hell were anxious to get their stranglehold on me and to be the controlling spirits in my life.

Thank God, Dobbs had come to town.

Thank God for the love of the people of the Baptist church. I started getting little notes passed along the pews to me during the morning services.

"Good to see you, Fay. Wait for me after the service. Love, Edna."

Edna Hadley was a daughter-in-law of one of the deacons; her husband was studying to be a pastor. We'd meet and she'd encourage me to attend some function or other with the young people. Best of all, she introduced me to her husband's mother and father. Every church needs a ministry like the one performed by the Hadleys at First Baptist. They kept a watchful, prayerful eye open each Sunday for those visiting in the congregation and made it a point of meeting and greeting them, and more often than not, inviting them home for what Mr. Hadley called a snack of "sardines on toast"! His wife would wink mischievously and the snack usually turned out to be Canadian roast beef in the British tradition, complete with Yorkshire puddin' and a dessert of home-baked pie. Given to hospitality, the Bible calls it!

I became a regular Sunday afternoon visitor to the Hadley home. After dinner we'd sit around and visit or share the Scriptures or just talk over the happenstances of the previous week. Here was direct, interested, personalized love.

I was having love written to me by D. J.; I was having it yelled in my ear through the lusty voice of Dobbs: "Blessed assurance, Jesus is mine; Oh, what a foretaste of glory divine. Heir of salvation, purchase of God; born of his Spirit, washed in his blood." I was having it preached to me from every pulpit I was exposed to, either at my own Baptist service or at the hell-fire-and-brimstone churches Dobbs dragged me into. I was seeing it through the Scriptures we studied at the youth groups: "You must be born again!"

"How can a man be born when he is old?" asked Nicodemus. "Can he enter the second time into his mother's womb, and be born?" (John 3:4).

Jesus answered, "Verily, verily, I say unto thee, except a man be born of water and of the Spirit, he cannot enter into the kingdom of God. That which is born of the flesh is flesh; and that which is born of the Spirit is spirit."

It seemed I had *not* been born again. Obviously, according to the words of Jesus himself, I could not enter into the Kingdom of God until I was. I knew I'd better get reborn and fast!

I had spent considerable time studying Zen Buddhism and various religions of the Far East—these were a complement to my cultural roots that dug deep into the earth of China. I read Lin Yutang and studied the proverbs of Confucius. I was intrigued with the theories of existentialism and any intellectual pursuit of the meaning of life. There was nowhere I could pigeonhole Jesus Christ.

He claimed to be Son of the living God, Lord of lords, King of kings, to the exclusion of anyone else. I had wrestled with the problems of his deity in the prison camp, walking the fine line of life and death.

"I am the way, the truth, and the life: no man cometh unto the Father, but by me. . . ." He was either a liar, deceiver, and charlatan, or he was all that he claimed to be. "Salvation is given by no other name . . ." he taught.

I had made my decision, by choice, by an act of my own will. I had chosen then to *believe*—now I chose to *receive*. There was no other alternative; I needed to appropriate that belief or reject it.

With the help of the Hadleys and Dr. Paul, I received Jesus Christ into my life and asked him to dwell in me, to live through me, and to regenerate me. I stepped over the threshold of faith into the Kingdom of God. I arranged to be baptized.

D. J. wrote "hallelujah!" Dobbs shouted "hallelujah!" And I squeaked a small, shaky "hallelujah" myself, realizing that something pretty important was happening to me. Just where it would take me or what that something involved I could not in my wildest dreams have imagined.

Baptism by immersion is a significant step of faith.

"I was baptized as a baby in the Roman Catholic faith," I told Mr. Hadley.

"Yes," he replied, "but that was an act of faith chosen for you by your parents. Now you have the opportunity of making your own decision. Symbolically through baptism the old life is dead and buried under the waters, and the new reborn life emerges, restored in Christ, resurrected in his righteousness. 'Old things are passed away and behold all things are become as new.' "

Jesus was baptized despite the protest of John the Baptist; could I do less?

I put on the white baptismal robe for immersion and stood waist-deep in the baptistry of the church. Dr. Paul had his right hand between the shoulder blades of my back and my own hands were clasping his left hand tightly.

"Upon public profession of your faith in Jesus Christ, I baptize you, Fay Westwood, in the name of the Father, the Son, and the Holy Ghost. Amen."

I arose from the waters, beaming, eager to claim my inheritance in the Kingdom of God. I had stepped through the door to abundant life.

"It is well, it is well with my soul," sang the choir.

"Now we are one in the spirit," said Dobbs, as he bent and kissed the palms of my hands.

FOUR
THE LEGACY

MR. HADLEY raced after me, down the twisting stairs from the
foyer to the girls' rest room.

"What's wrong, Fay?"

The tears were streaming down my face and a knot of emotion
was so tight in my chest that I thought I'd turn blue and burst
before I could choke out the sobs.

"Something's happened to my father. . . . Oh, Mr. Hadley, I
don't know what it is, but I know something has happened to
him!"

In the middle of the Sunday service, just before the offertory,
Father's presence had stood beside me and the call "Snooky,
Snooky!" had interjected my meditations with desperate clarity.
The anxiety persisted and the childhood nickname, used only by
my father, kept ringing in my ears, so much so that before my self-
control broke I rushed out of the sanctuary.

Mr. Hadley steadied me and gently eased me down on the couch
beside him. Pulling a handkerchief out of his breast pocket, he
dried my eyes and knit his brows together in a perplexed frown.
He took my hands in his.

"God knows exactly where your father is and what he is doing
right now, Fay. Why don't we just take him before our Lord in
prayer!"

I buried my head in my hands. Crying quietly, I tried to follow the words of Mr. Hadley's prayer while my heart drifted miles away, searching out possibilities of tragedy. What was it one of Shakespeare's characters said . . . "My words fly up, my thoughts remain below. Words without thoughts never to heaven go."

"Forgive me, Lord," I whispered.

Mr. Hadley's prayer continued, ". . . and Father, I thank you that you created Ernest Westwood, that you gave him life, that he is made in your image and in your likeness. I thank you that you know the totality of him—his entire self—that you know his thoughts and the depth of his heart. Thank you that he was the channel through which you chose to give us Fay. Wherever he is and whatever is the need of his life at this hour, we present him to you, and trust him to you, and ask that you bless him, and keep him in your infinite mercy and love. We pray for his salvation, that he will know and receive Jesus Christ as Lord and Savior, and this we pray in perfect confidence, assured that it is your will that none should perish. So we thank you; under the authority of the name of Jesus Christ, through whose righteousness we come before you. Amen."

"Amen," I sniffed.

The telegram arrived from Australia the next morning.

"Sorry to inform you Ernest died of cancer today. Details following." It was signed by his brother Percy.

When Father was thirteen, a schoolboy at the famous missionary school in Chefoo, China, he had written his own epitaph:

Here lies E. W. W.
Who no longer will troubleyou, troubleyou!

My father was dead.

"Your Stranger Daddy." That's how he had signed all his letters. How little we knew each other and how desperately we wanted to know each other, to love each other, to share our joy of words, to rhyme verses together, to talk of sea and wind and stars. I yearned to be held tight against his chest and have him stroke my hair and whisper, "My little girl!"

True to the disciplines of her Roman Catholic faith, my mother had not considered divorce, but separation had been inevitable. My parents had many years of intermittent happiness together, but finally the irresponsibility of my father's life brought irreconcilable differences into their marriage. With two young, impressionable children to consider, my mother had to choose the heartbreak of separation from a man she loved. I was seven years old at the time.

The memories of my father were limited to those occasions when he had come home and, bounding into the room where I was hiding (generally behind a sofa or chair, waiting to pounce on him), he'd call "Snooky? Snooky? Where are you—I know you're in here somewhere!"

I'd jump him and he'd catch me in his arms and toss me high above his head while we both giggled and laughed our way through the romp.

The only tangible remembrance I had of him was the beautiful little French bisque doll that sat in its place of honor on my dresser. He had visited me at the convent school in Tsingtao one summer and brought the elegant gift.

I was the envy of the school as I showed off my treasure. She had a piquant, provocative look, and her blue eyes were heavily lashed. She came with a complete wardrobe of dresses stitched in exquisite French laces and beribboned silks. Her tiny hands were tucked into a white ermine muff and a saucy white fur hat balanced precariously on her carefully coiffured head. She had long slender French legs and painted high heeled shoes on tiny feet. From tip to toe she was exquisitely crafted.

Dad took me sailing off the beach at Tsingtao that summer. His blond hair was tousled by the wind and his smoky eyes caught the sunlight as we yawed against the breakers. Those eyes held caverns of changing shadows. He belonged in Shangri-la, this Stranger Daddy, in a world that never was. He stepped in and out of my childhood like a ghost of dynasties past—elusive and unpredictable.

His command of words held me in stunned captivity and I'd listen in awe as he worked out the verses of a poem . . .

"How's this, Snooks? 'Canvas leaning taut in splendor, heeling to the cloudy thunder of the blue waves. . . .'"

"Wonderful!" I'd gasp, and then he'd urge me on to express myself in a couplet or two. We also wrote some poetry together that summer.

"Condense, be graphic, and eliminate the irrelevant; let that be a guideline in all your writing, Kitten—go for it, you have the sensitivity."

His letters scattered themselves through my years. He frequently enclosed clippings of his poems and articles, many of which were published in the Australian newspapers. These became the only insights I had into the personality and character of my Stranger Daddy.

"Pray for your father," my mother said every night before I went to bed.

He had drifted away from the roots of faith that had brought his parents out to China in the first place. They had arrived from Australia in 1892, the time of Hudson Taylor, and set up a CIM base in one of the northern provinces.

As I prayed for my father nightly, I'm sure that his parents, then retired in Australia, prayed for him also. With David they could groan, "Oh, Absalom, my son, my son!" The most difficult burden of those of the faith is to lose a child to the ways of the world. They continued to wrestle for his soul.

I did not expect my father ever to reconcile his life to God. I prayed with a sense of duty and obligation, begging God for his merciful intercession, but I did not pray in faith believing. I prayed in doubt, hesitating, and through that doubt was to learn of the compassionate loving-kindness of God the Father—loving-kindness that transcended human frailty.

"Forgive this awful scrawl, Snooks," Dad wrote from his prison camp in Hong Kong, "but I'm almost blind."

The war, the Japanese invasion, the battle of Repulse Bay . . . the action-packed role of an officer with the Royal Navy . . . the machine guns. "Cut their stinking throats," he'd shouted. The bloodied bodies of his comrades. Then the capture and internment.

Starvation . . . the sickness of the camp . . . the bloated bodies of the Chinese children as they lined the barbed wire hoping to share in some morsel of the rations of the prisoners of war . . . rice grains scoured from garbage cans . . . diphtheria and two hundred dead, buried in the waste ground in the hills. Years of endurance. Then the final *victory*!

No repentance, no prayer or need of God, no benediction of thanks from this man of words and steel, only the explosion back into his stream of life — with a difference! His health was broken. Weighing ninety pounds upon his release, he watched companions die on the ferry home; one weighed only forty-five pounds.

"I've been through hell," he wrote. "I got callous in that bloody camp and now I don't seem able to unfreeze. . . ."

The last letter I had from him was written from a hospital in Hong Kong where he had been taken after a severe heart attack. He was going home, home to Australia, home on doctors' orders to reconstruct his life.

"Modified, no more high spots! A forest service job, perhaps, and quietness," he wrote. "Snooks, I think of you incessantly these nights."

"Yes, it is strange," Mr. Hadley was saying. "On Sunday when you heard his voice and felt his presence, his last dying thoughts must surely have been with you."

I was having dinner with the Hadleys a week after the telegram. They had come and offered their condolences to my mother and left a beautiful bouquet of flowers as token of their sympathy and love.

Now I was telling them just how dearly I had missed having a father in my life, my resentments of my dad's lack of responsibility, and yet my admiration for his free spirit and adventuresome life style. In retrospect his life read like that of the hero in some

Ernest Hemingway novel—lusty, gusty, and action-packed, with all the concomitant sorrows.

"What you need to realize, Fay," continued Mr. Hadley, "is that God is your Father. Jesus taught us this in the Lord's prayer: 'Our *Father* who art in heaven.' Before you were born, God was your Father; God was your father's Father; God will be your children's Father. Speak to him as Father. Know him as Father. He will never let you down; you are daughter of the greatest Father that ever was or ever will be. He is your 'Abba' Father, your Daddy Father, your personalized Father and he loves you more than any mortal mother or father or anyone else ever could. Saturate yourself with that knowledge, and appropriate it."

That night as I went to my prayers I said experimentally "My Daddy who is in heaven, hallowed be your name, your Kingdom come. . . ." I felt his loving arms around me, and I almost heard him say "My little girl . . ."

Many weeks later Mother and I sat on the floor going carefully through the contents of the small suitcase. It had arrived from Hobart and contained the pathetic totality of my father's possessions: his books of minutely scrawled notes, many of them made while incarcerated, his papers, and then . . . the exciting discovery of a large black book, *The Holy Bible in Modern English*. I took it carefully in my hands and opened it slowly. Pasted on the inside cover was a baptismal certificate with a picture of an artist's conception of the baptism of Jesus.

"Buried with him in baptism" (Col. 2:12)

Name: Ernest William Westwood

Romans 6:1-6: What shall we say then? Shall we continue in sin, that grace may abound? God forbid. How shall we, that are dead to sin, live any longer therein? Know ye not, that so many of us as were baptized into Jesus Christ were baptized into his death? Therefore we are buried with him by baptism into death: that like as Christ was raised up from the dead by the glory of the Father, even so we also should walk in newness of life. For if we have been planted together in the likeness of his death, we shall be also in the likeness of his resurrection. Knowing this, that our old man is crucified with him, that the body of sin might be destroyed, that henceforth we should not serve sin.

Baptized by: Stanley J. Morrow
National Revival Crusade—Sydney

My father had been baptized! My father had come forward at a National Revival Crusade in Australia, had repented of his sins, and had accepted Jesus Christ as his Lord and Savior! My father had been baptized before he died!

I fairly whooped around the room and my mother sat in prayerful thanksgiving, the tears streaming down her face.

"Wait till the Hadleys hear about this," I hollered.

Eagerly I thumbed through the notebooks. In the front of each one was written in a practically illegible scrawl: "What hast thou that thou didst not receive?" (1 Cor. 4:7).

Then a quotation of Sir Francis Drake: "Men pass away but people abide. See that ye hold fast the heritage we leave you. Yea, and teach your children its value, that never in the coming centuries their hearts may fail them or their hands grow weak. Hitherto we have been too much afraid. Henceforth we will fear only God."

This was followed by a prayer of the famous British admiral, dated 1587: "Oh Lord God, when Thou givest to Thy servants to endeavor any great matter, grant us to know that it is not the beginning but the continuing of the same until it be thoroughly finished which yieldeth the true glory; through Him who for the finishing of Thy work laid down His life, our Redeemer, Jesus Christ. Amen."

The papers yielded up even more praise—a full correspondence with the astronomer of the Adelaide Observatory. My father had apparently developed a deep friendship with him, kindled by his avid interest in the stars. In the midst of all the technical observations of the constellations, was one gem of a letter.

Adelaide Observatory
Adelaide, South Australia

My dear Ernest,

I am doubly indebted to you for your two letters, which I have very thankfully received together with the two sets of very interesting and helpful notes, which I am reading several times to get the full benefit from them.

I hope you will have all your collection of notes published some time. I am sure there will be a great number of readers in these times who will be glad to read them. I wanted to say at the start that your letters and notes are very soul-satisfying; and in saying that, I am thinking that what gives us the deepest satisfaction is the Word of God.

The Living Word, in our hearts, the written Word in the Bible, and the spoken Word, conveying divine messages of comfort and help . . . all are united. "Man shall not live by bread alone, but by every word which proceedeth out of the mouth of God."

So this word of God and everything which can throw light and make it clear to us, is vital for our welfare. I am very glad therefore that we have met, for we have much to share together in these great things.

By a coincidence my brother's name is Ernest, and in the friendship which has now been given to us we have established the wider relationship spoken of by Christ when He said "Whosoever shall do the will of God, the same is my brother, and my sister, and my mother."

My wife was greatly interested in the commentary you gave us on the 23rd Psalm, and joins her thanks with mine to you.

That was very interesting about Moffatt's translation of 1 Corinthians 2 concerning the "hidden wisdom." Far beyond the knowledge of all worldly matters of art, literature, or science, is the knowledge of God. The fulfillment of this great quest, we are promised, is to be the universal experience in the coming age when Jeremiah tells us "they shall teach no more every man his neighbor, and every man his brother, saying Know the Lord, for they shall all know me, from the least of them unto the greatest of them, saith the Lord."

I am just at the point of writing to astronomical friends in the U.S.A., Great Britain, and France to get some words of encouragement for the Town Hall meeting which I hope to arrange early in April to bring about

a restoration of our Adelaide Observatory. I must close now. "The grace of our Lord Jesus Christ be with you always."
Yours,
George

I wondered if "George" had visited him as he was dying. God in his loving-kindness had put a spiritual brother beside him to strengthen and comfort him in his full commitment to Jesus Christ and study of the Bible. The brooding heartache of my father's loneliness was eased and I breathed a quiet "Thank you, George!"

I spent hours going through the scrapbooks of inspirational clippings; notebooks relating to Dad's personal response to the Scriptures. I found poems and prayers glowing in their tribute to his faith in the living God, all painstakingly written in a tiny script that clearly showed my father was indeed going blind.

Years before he had written: "The mind can in its white hot moments purge any vision of its dross." Wrong, I thought, "The *soul* can in its white hot moments purge the *mind* of all its dross."

Through the intercession of the Holy Spirit of God, his soul, his mind, and his entire life had been purged; the dross sifted away and the pure alloy of his faith revealed.

I stopped a moment and listened. The doves had long ceased their billing and cooing under the eaves and the domestic noises of neighbors getting ready for bed were silenced. Only the rhythmic ticking of the clock beat a steady tempo: "He-lives, he-lives, he-lives, he-lives. . . ." My father was alive and well with Jesus Christ. From that moment on, death spelled victory in my vocabulary. My father had entered eternal life.

God took the doubt, the nonbelieving prayers, the resentment and despair of my growing years and said "With me, *all* things are possible!"

It was after midnight. I stacked the books and papers carefully; they were little more than an armload. This was my legacy from my father. Of no commercial value, it was indeed a legacy that money couldn't buy. It was a legacy that through the years would pay immortal dividends.

FIVE
TO LOVE AND TO CHERISH

THERE IT WAS again, shrill and persistent! There was no doubt about it this time, it *was* the doorbell. I groped on the night stand for my watch. Eleven-thirty—who on earth would be calling on us at this hour?

"Buz-z-z, buz-z-z-z!" For heaven's sake, I thought, get your finger off it, I'm coming!

Sleepily I rolled out of bed, trying not to disturb the prone figure of my mother. The one thing I hated about our move to the new apartment was the fact that we had to share a double bed. I was a fidgety, restless sleeper. "Stop it, Bubs," she'd say. "If you move once more I'm going to pinch you!"

I'd lie there for seemingly interminable moments, aching to roll over, or bend a knee or elbow. My ballet exercises frequently gave me muscle twitches and my tossing and moving about resulted in pinches that made bedtime a vexing experience.

Pulling on a kimono, I stumbled to the door and threw it open without bothering to switch on the hallway light.

A red and black Pendleton shirt collided with my eye level, and a pair of heavy logger's boots came within inches of treading on my bare toes. In a daze, I looked up. Paul Bunyan himself! A tall, husky man towered above me. He rubbed his fingers through a head full of platinum curls and peered down at me through heavy rimmed glasses. "Say, I'm sorry!" he apologized. "I thought this was my sister Jean's apartment."

Jean, the singer next door. Beautiful and talented, she spent the summer months with Vancouver's popular Theatre Under the Stars in Stanley Park. We had seen her perform in "The Desert Song," "The Pirates of Penzance," and other musicals. We listened daily to her practicing favorite operatic arias through the thin walls that separated our bedrooms. So this was her brother.

With typical femininity my first thought was, "Good grief, why didn't I take a moment to at least comb out my tousled hair?"

"Jean lives next door," I explained, "but she's singing tonight. Would you care to come in for a cup of tea and wait for her here?"

"Thanks, no, I feel badly at having bothered you. I'm John Angus. I just got off the boat from Port Alberni. I'll go on down and get a cup of coffee on Robson Street and catch her after the show. Maybe, if you don't mind, though, I could leave my suitcase here and pick it up in the morning."

He tossed his suitcase into the hallway and then was off, turning back with a shy grin to wave his goodbye.

Curious man, I thought. Tall, rugged, different . . . interesting. John Angus, eh? I liked the name. Angus made me think of swirling kilts, hairy chests, and tam-o'-shanters bobbing to the pitch of bagpipes.

I crept back into bed and listened to the traffic rolling down Robson Street until the wee hours of the morning.

We were sharing an apartment with an elderly lady named Mrs. Peters. She owned the furniture, and in order to help meet her expenses she rented out the living room and dining room of her one bedroom suite. The high archway that separated our two rooms was draped with heavy blue velvet curtains. These were left open during the day to let in the sunlight from the bay window of what was now our bedroom, and pulled closed at night to tuck us into privacy. We shared the kitchen and bath, and although it was dark, it was an improvement over Alberni Street's closet-with-hotplate kitchen and interminable trips to the bathroom to wash the dishes. Here at least we had a full stove with an oven and sink. Thank God for small mercies.

Mrs. Peters had two obvious vices: whist and the race horses. She'd go out several nights a week and gamble at the whist games. During the racing season she made frequent trips to Lansdowne Park to place her bets. This generally led to disaster in her finances. When funds got low, she'd move a portable cot into the kitchen and take up residence alongside the fumes of the gas stove, while she rented out her bedroom for more income. It was a most unsatisfactory arrangement for us, as that meant we had to make room for a fourth person in the apartment.

"Don't worry, Mrs. Westwood," Peters would say, "it won't be for long; my luck will turn and then I'll get my bedroom back."

She had been widowed years ago and had suffered through the agony of losing a five-year-old daughter to cancer. "She'd scream and scream until she'd pass out," Peters would tell us, the tears streaming down her face. "The cancer was all through her. All I could do was hold her while she got more and more bloated—she died in my arms, she did." A picture of the sad-eyed little girl hung in the hallway, her swollen body bursting out of its organdy pinafore.

The furniture in the apartment was of good quality and Mrs. Peters must have, at some time in her life, come from a home of comfort. It was tragic to see her sleeping in the kitchen. She moved about like a well-rounded brown mole, her dark eyes squinting through thick lenses as though they were unaccustomed to the daylight. She seemed content with the routines she had cut out for herself and was always very kind to us, rapping on our door to share a cup of tea or a homemade treat, hot out of her oven.

I could relate well to her adversity. Through the years we had been spun around quite severely ourselves. As I took a leisurely bath that morning, under the crossed strings of damp laundry hanging from brackets around me, I was strangely amused to find ourselves such a long cry from the servants and grandeur of our life in the Far East. I had taken quite a tumble from the "Young Missy" status of the Colonial Empire. We had survived the mucky years of concentration camp, and now Mother and I found ourselves merging into the stream of the hard-working middle classes.

John Angus came by for his suitcase.

"Say, Fay, how about dinner and a show tonight? I'm only going to be in town for the weekend, then I'm going to the World Series." There was excitement in his voice.

The World Series? Baseball? What kind of a guy was this, I wondered, who would spend all that money just to go to New York to see a few baseball games!

He was transformed when he picked me up that evening. The natty beige gabardine suit, with cream-colored, french-cuffed shirt and silk tie, was a far cry from the logging boots. He had money in his pockets and he was willing to spend it. We dined in style. Somehow I felt I did not have to watch the menu prices with John as I did with so many of my other escorts.

He brought a new dimension to my experience and I kept asking him to tell me more about the tall trees and lumberjacks of the logging camp. He had just worked there for the summer, making as much money as he could, as fast as he could.

"The cardinal sin was to talk during meals," he said as we dug our knives into a juicy steak. "Nobody talked—I mean, you just ate, and ate lots! Oatmeal, ham, eggs, sausages, pancakes, milk, coffee, the works for breakfast; those guys could sure pack it in!"

He waved his fork around to emphasize the point and I noticed his long slender fingers and narrow wrists; they were delicate, sensitive hands—the type that should belong to a surgeon, not to be calloused by the peavy (hook) that pulled the heavy logs into a floating boom.

"Each had his own favorite place at the food tables. It was like a sacred ritual, and nobody else had better ever sit in that place. There was this huge French Canadian rigger. The first day on the job I went in to breakfast and sat in his place. Every knife and fork stopped and forty pairs of eyes followed him as he came up behind me. At first I thought he was going to pick me up by the scruff of my neck and throw me across the room. That's what they did, y'know. Well, he looked hard at me, realized I was a greenhorn, and then moved on to the next table, never saying a word. Boy, did I get out of there fast! At all the meals after that I made sure I was one of the last to sit down."

The thought of anyone throwing this six-foot, broad-shouldered hulk of a man across a room was inconceivable to me! Guess they toughened up at the logging camps.

After the show we walked home arm in arm. Somehow we didn't want to let go of the night. The crisp, moist Vancouver night air brought roses into our cheeks and gave us a second wind. After we got to the apartment building we decided to walk around the block again, and then once again, and then around a few more blocks, laughing and chatting. I was mainly the one chatting. John was a quiet man, easy to be with, and I had to draw him out by questions, questions, and more questions. I was fascinated with the yarns of back-riggers digging their climbing irons foot over foot to top the spar tree; chokermen, fallers, and buckers—I was learning a whole new vocabulary!

I liked him.

The next day was Sunday. "Do you ever go to church?" I asked.

"Yeah, sure, sometimes."

"Would you like to go with me tomorrow morning?"

"Sure, Babe." He had dropped the Fay, and I was now "Babe," or "Hon," something else to get used to.

"Are you a Christian, John?"

"Yeah, sure."

"I mean, do you believe in Jesus Christ?"

"Sure, Babe! Why? Something bothering you?"

He believed in God, he believed in Jesus Christ—his faith was that concrete.

After church we rented bicycles and rode around the circumference of Stanley Park, stopping at various scenic points to inhale the breathtaking view. Snow-capped mountains, towering Douglas firs, and wind-chopped ocean—Vancouver on a bright, sunny day was one step from Paradise.

We cycled past the strip of beach at English Bay where Dobbs and I had spent so much time together and I wondered what it

would be like to lie wrapped in a blanket on the sands with John.
It was November before I saw him again. He arrived in a large
two-toned green Nash with reclining seats, waving tickets to the
local Canucks hockey game. I had loved grass hockey and played
right wing on the Vancouver all-star girls' team. It was fast action
with an emphasis on coordination, accuracy, and speed. Ice hockey
was even more so, with the added stimulation of bodies crashing
against the boards and many bloodied noses. Sitting close to the
ice, we yelled ourselves hoarse.

By Christmas we were dating steadily.

"Let's go up into the mountains of West Van and cut our own
tree," suggested John. Out came the logger's boots, the Pendleton
shirt, and a hatchet. We drove as high as we could, then trekked
into the wonderland of trees laden with snow. It was Act II of *The
Nutcracker* ballet, the Snow Queen's Palace, in real life! Huffing
and puffing, I followed in the trail of the big boots until I thought
my lungs would burst.

"That's it," I gasped. "We'll have to find one here, I just can't
hike any further."

"No, Babe, none of these will do," said the voice of the expert,
and with an effortless motion he picked me up and carried me a
few more hundred yards.

"That's it, over there," he pointed, and told me how the timber
cruisers of the logging camps would go around marking the trees to
be felled.

I sat on a large rock and admired his strength and skill as his
muscles rippled around his shoulder blades. He chopped down
the tree. Then, dragging it behind him, he sat down. He pulled me
onto his knee and we sat huddled in the snow, leaning against the
fresh, prickly branches of a small Douglas fir.

"I love you, Fay," he whispered as he cupped my face in those
sensitive hands.

"I cherish you. You are the dearest and most valuable thing that
has ever come into my life. My whole world has changed. I have
nothing to offer you now, but one day I will have, and then I'm
coming back and I'm gonna marry you! I don't ever want anyone

else but you, understand?" He gave me a little shake to emphasize the point.

"Never anyone but you! Don't you forget that!"

I had been loved, but I had never before been told that I was cherished, that I was treasured, that I was valued above everything and everyone else.

Dobbs expected me to fit snugly into the plan of *his* life, according to the direction of *his* life; now here was a man who wanted to make *me* the direction of his life and build that life around *my* happiness.

The tears came into my eyes. "Thank you, John," I murmured, "I will remember that, always; give me time to think."

I sat sheltered in his arms in the snow forest, the silence broken only by the odd flutter of wings as birds started bedding down for the night.

The sun was dipping over the horizon and long shadows stretched across the trail of our footsteps as we trudged downhill.

A parcel had arrived from an armed forces station. The notice said I needed to go down to pick it up.

Standing at the window of the post office, I ripped open the brown paper wrapping and disclosed a beautiful long jeweler's box covered in royal blue velvet. Both the postal clerk and I gasped as I opened it: moonstones—beautiful, pale, cloudy blue moonstones set in a necklace, bracelet, and earrings. They seemed lifeless as they lay there, but the moment I lifted them out the light shimmered through their translucence and fired them with brilliance.

"Happy Christmas, Darling," the card read, signed *"Dobbs."*

"Ninety dollars in customs tariff due," said the clerk.

"Ninety dollars? I don't have ninety dollars!"

"Sorry about that, Miss."

"What are you going to do with them?" I asked as he bundled the parcel back up.

"No option. Send them back," said the clerk.

I burst into tears and sobbed, "How can you send them back?

These are from my boyfriend, fighting in Korea. How can you send them back, what will he think?"

"Ninety dollars," said the clerk.

By then I was boo-hooing loudly all over the place, running out of tissues and making an utter scene. The postmaster came out of his office and, appraising the sincerity of my heartbreak, quietly and carefully stamped the parcel "passed—duty-free."

I had never had anything quite so beautiful. I wore them on New Year's Eve. John took me dancing at the Panorama Roof on top of the Vancouver Hotel. We brought in the New Year together, shuffling around the crowded ballroom floor while Giselle MacKenzie sang "Should Olde Acquaintance Be Forgot."

A stab of guilt cut through me as I fingered the moonstones. I pictured Dobbs in army barracks reading his Bible, praying for me, as I danced cheek-to-cheek with this tall, blond Canadian.

SIX
TO HAVE AND TO HOLD

TIME MEASURED in moments . . . the inescapable laser of memory that probes the blood to run hot or cold.

It was the first time I had seen Dobbs in his army khakis! The red of his hair dulled to a tawny amber in contrast.

"It's so good to be home, Darling, so good to be home!"

He crushed me to him and the brass buttons on his jacket cut into the softness of my body. I flinched, and had a moment of panic as I remembered another uniform on another GI, in China, just after the war. The brass buttons on his jacket, too, had cut into me, and his mouth had clamped on mine and he had pinned me down atop a ledge on a roof garden. I could still taste the blood in my mouth and feel the fumbling fingers ripping off my skirt. The horror of the attempted rape sent a wave of nausea through me.

"This is Dobbs," I had to remind myself as I yielded to the pressure of his embrace.

The years had filled him out in a metamorphosis from boy to man. The hollow cheeks were now rounded and I felt a new solidarity in his body as he held me; a new authority, a new determination. The hesitancy of his first love had matured into the demands of long-restrained passion.

"Don't talk," he whispered, "don't talk! Two years I've waited for this moment. Two years I've dreamed and prayed. I just want to hold you for endless time. . . ."

His words breathed ripples through my hair and I tucked my mouth against the nape of his neck as he cradled my head.

We stood there in the doorway, swaying gently back and forth, rocking our togetherness to close the spaces of the years. A strange urgency swept over him as at last he said, "Let's go," and his eyes searched my face hungrily.

He had bought an old Chevy, and we drove to park at our favorite beach at English Bay. A wave of nostalgic regret brought the tears into my eyes as I realized that no longer would we need to roll up in the black and red plaid blanket, huddled together on the sands. We had our own chariot now, our place of privacy away from prying eyes and the biting night air.

It was an evening of long silences—healing silences, broken only by the guttural anger of his war reminiscences.

"The burns—" he said, "napalm wiped out men's bodies; sometimes it was our own planes that sprayed them by mistake!"

"Blessed be the peacemakers," I whispered, "for they shall be called the children of God!"

He took me home in the wee hours of the morning.

"He's suffered," I thought, "a different sort of suffering from concentration camp—a horrible anguish as he saw the body-maiming, grotesque casualties of combat."

"This is not the time to tell him about John," I resolved guiltily.

Thank God for friends who fill the gaps.

The brethren at the Tabernacle held a special service of rejoicing for the safe return of Dobbs and it was not long before we were once again in the swim of fellowships, beach parties, and Bible studies.

He brought me home a rolled-up silken scroll.

"Open it up," he said, grinning mischievously. I unraveled my portrait, colorfully painted on silk by a Chinese artist, copied from a snap I had enclosed in one of my letters.

"I had two done," he said. "One hung by my bunk through the whole stay over there, and this other—I had it done for you."

"Why, Dobbs," I said, "I look Chinese!"

Sure enough, the artist in his endeavor to improve the portrait had given me the slanted eyes and jet black hair which to him were the epitome of beauty.

We had a good laugh, and once again rehashed our early beginnings—not *his* war, in Korea, but *our* war, in the concentration camp at Yangchow.

Letters and flowers were arriving regularly from John. His family had moved to Spokane and he was immersed in his studies at Washington State University, waiting impatiently for a semester break when he could rush up to Vancouver.

My loyalty to Dobbs was fierce. I owed so much to him, but I knew in my heart of hearts that I didn't want to marry him. I did what any sensitive woman would do; I tossed through sleepless nights and pounded my pillow with frustration. I wept guilty tears, I worried, and I grew pale and thin. I made excuses and avoided seeing Dobbs as much as I could. He was making plans for his own future and the serious decision of whether to settle in the United States or locate permanently in Canada.

A confrontation was inevitable, and I guess it came one evening when my kisses must have lacked their usual zip and zest. I was getting nervous and I was starting to show it.

"Everything's not OK," he was saying. We were parked in front of the apartment, ready to say good night. "Something has been bugging you for weeks. What is it?"

I looked down and blew my nose.

"Fay, do you still love me?"

"Oh, yes, Dobbs, you know that! I'll always love you!"

He thought for a moment as he watched me snivel. "Is there somebody else?"

"No," I lied, still looking down.

A terrible whiteness pinched his face and drew his lips together into a thin line. "Don't you lie to me, Fay! Don't you ever lie to me."

His hands gripped my face and tilted it upward so that I could not avoid looking directly into those penetrating blue eyes.

Somehow it was like looking right into the face of God!

I told him about John.

He walked me to the apartment.

With his eyes brimming, he quietly said, "God bless you, Fay," kissing me gently. Then he spun on his heels and walked out of my life.

I felt bereft. By deliberate choice I had severed someone who had brought into my life goodness, honor, and godly love, someone who had shared with me memories that I would live and die with. Someone who had given me courage and strength in my moments of despair and weakness. Someone so special that he could never be forgotten or replaced—someone with whom I didn't want to live, yet could not tolerate the thought of living without!

For weeks I grieved the grief of death. I read and reread his letters and muddled over mementos and pictures.

To ease the heartache I flew into a whirlwind of activity, dating as many different men as frequently as possible. I shunned the deeper relationships and lived on the surface of my emotions.

John became jealous and furious. Eventually he got fed up with my shilly-shallying around, and on his graduation from Washington State with a B.Sc. in Engineering, he sent me this telegram:

DEAR FAY ARRIVING TOMORROW CANCEL COMMITMENTS UNCERTAINTIES PREVENTED EARLIER NOTIFICATION LOVE JOHN

The nerve of him, I thought, telling me to cancel my commitments. As it happened I had made elaborate plans for a party with friends at Vancouver's choice Georgia Hotel; it was a special occasion.

I managed to squirm out of my date by telling him that an old friend of the family was coming into town. I got Jim a date with a pretty little English girl, and I waited for John—or rather we all did, as we had planned to go to the party as a group. Finally he arrived, beaming with anticipation, and lifted me off my feet to kiss me. Jim looked rather unhappy and I'm sure I looked rather confused.

That weekend I got the ultimatum.

"I'm going down to Los Angeles to work as a civil engineer with
the County Flood Control. I won't be able to keep coming up here
the way I've been doing over the past months. I can't wait any
longer—marry me!"

"Will you give me another year?" I whined.

"No. I love you; I've never loved anyone else and I don't want
anyone else, *but* I've also given you enough time. Marry me, and if
you won't, then I'll just have to go off and find someone who will!"

I was very reluctant to get married. I was feeling more and more
independent and was even saving a portion of my meager salary for
a trip to England. But the thought that if I didn't marry this tall,
handsome Canadian, he'd go off and find someone else who
would, rattled me to the core!

He gave me one week to make my decision.

It was a week on my knees and it was a week of turmoil. I didn't
particularly want to marry him right now, but then I didn't want
anyone else to marry him either; he was MINE!

"O God," I prayed, "the thought of living with any one man for
the rest of my life frightens me half to death! I don't have the
wisdom to choose for myself. Please make this choice for me!"

The more I prayed, the more at peace I felt about marrying John.
I took the plunge and said YES!

I thought John had fainted at the other end of the long-distance
call, there was such a long pause before his exuberance!

I wrote to D. J. Watson immediately and here's the letter he sent
in reply:

Selly Oak,
Birmingham, England
My dear Fay,
    It is a good job that I have passed through so many crises in China and
elsewhere—so many wars and bombings and rumors of wars, otherwise I
might be bowled off my feet with shock. As it is, I'm not. I hasten to
congratulate . . . John, at least on gaining YOU! If I knew just a bit more
about John (whose name I remember but not much more) I might
congratulate you on having JOHN!
    It has been rather a job for my ordinary mind to keep tabs on all the

*young men in and out of your life, but you certainly appear to be able to
reciprocate John's love, and if your mother is happier over him than over
any of the others, then I am relieved and glad. You can tell her that I trust
her judgment as well as yours.*

*I only hope that John is a thorough Christian fellow, because mere
nominal Christianity—of which there is such a lot around nowadays—is
the ruin of lots of homes and lives. When I say Christian I don't want
him to be rather pie-in-the-sky, with a text for every occasion, but some
belief and principle in his mind and heart about God and life, and a
commitment to Jesus Christ as Savior and Lord.*

*If he hasn't fully got there, then you must help him, dear Lassie, so that
Christ will always be the Lord of your home. Connect up with some
church that is really alive (not mere numbers) wherever you go. I pray for
you daily.*

Love,

D. J. Watson

As John had just started his new job and could not take any time
off, we decided that I would fly down to Los Angeles over the
Easter weekend.

I loved the flight! From the first moment I felt the exhilaration of
soaring high above the clouds and watched the world below shrink
in proportion, I knew this was to be a natural affinity. Flying
developed in me a perspective on the universe that has never failed
to leave me breathless and completely in awe.

As we broke through the clouds and banked around the L.A.
basin, it stretched as far as the eye could see—City of the Angels! I
breathed a sigh of relief as I saw the mountains; somehow I have
always needed to "lift up mine eyes unto the hills." They were not
lush and green like the Canadian forests, but they dominated the
skyline, writing a bold signature over the valley. Like Alice, I felt I
was stepping through a looking glass into Wonderland.

"Dear Father," I thought, "you've brought me a long way from
the muddy waters of the Wangpoo Creek!"

John's curly head towered above the waiting crowd. He was
deeply tanned and I liked the way his belt hugged his trim waist.

"A gorgeous hunk o' man," my girl friends had called him. They were right!

He lifted me off my feet in an enormous hug and we giggled and laughed our way out of the airport.

"Babe, have I got an evening planned for you!" he said.

I had a hunch that a diamond was burning its way through one of his pockets and I wondered just where he'd take me to slip it on my finger.

We had the traditional candlelit dinner in a romantic setting; then he drove up and up, and 'round and 'round the famous Griffith Park.

"I'm taking you as close to heaven as I can get you," he grinned.

Sure enough, we went all the way up to the Griffith Park Observatory; all the way up the stairs of the Planetarium to the terrace at the top where, under the winking stars, he pledged me his troth! A beautiful ring—five diamonds in a row which glistened blue-white in the moonlight and sent a flush of pleasure through me.

"We're spending Easter Sunday at the San Juan Capistrano Mission," he said, and launched into a historical background of all the missions in California.

"One day we'll visit them all—you're gonna love it down here!"

Arm in arm, and heart in heart, we walked the paths of San Juan Capistrano and took pictures of each other in front of the mission bells. We made our wedding plans there, in those sanctified gardens, and knelt in wide-eyed wonder in the beautiful chapel. I felt cloistered and completely at home as memories transported me back to the chapel of the Sacred Heart Convent in Shanghai where I had made my first holy communion! Reverend Mother Genee, Mére Alfreda, and Soeur Cecile would be pleased, I thought, that I had taken time in the weekend of my betrothal to kneel before the Eucharist—as though I were still a child of the Sacred Heart.

John and I were married on September 3 in Vancouver, British Columbia, at Trinity Baptist Church. It was a traditional English wedding.

As I walked down the aisle on the arm of my Uncle Bill, John, waiting at the foot of the altar, looked like a youthful member of the House of Lords. His pin-striped trousers and cut-away coat added stature to his height. He smiled and his eyes drew me to him all the way.

I, Fay, take thee John, to be my wedded husband, to have and to hold from this day forward, for better for worse, for richer for poorer, in sickness and in health, to love and to cherish, till death us do part, according to God's holy ordinance; and thereto I pledge thee my troth.

Yes, on a clear day, Vancouver *is* one step from Paradise! Sleeping Beauty Ridge and the Twin Lions looked deep purple in the shadows of the afternoon, and the sun bounced crystal prisms off the choppy waters of English Bay as we drove to the famous Yacht Club for the reception.

Mr. Hadley proposed the toast to the bride and said he knew that I would bring into my marriage the same zest and enthusiasm that was characteristic of my *joie de vivre!*

John's hand shook with nervousness as he prepared to respond and to toast the bridesmaids. I muttered out of the side of my mouth, "If you're going to spill your drink, aim it away from my dress!"

He had promised me a wedding night at Victoria's Empress Hotel in its picturesque English setting on Vancouver Island.

"Violins will serenade us through dinner, Honey," he'd said, "and we'll have tea and crumpets down in the conservatory!"

The rest of the week of our honeymoon was booked into a beachside cottage at Point-No-Point, a resort at a bend in the Island that faced right into the surf of the Pacific Ocean. The brochure showed witches' cauldrons of white water churning around the rocks of a rugged coastline. The dining room featured home-cooked meals, and as an interesting sideline the owners bred Siamese cats!

"The surf will come thundering up practically to the foot of your bed," the travel agent had told us. "It is private and quiet and you'll enjoy walking down to explore the abandoned lighthouse at the point."

John's old green Nash squeaked its way into the hold of the ferry as we boarded from Horseshoe Bay, and we spent much of the ride across the Sound arm in arm, the wind whipping our hair as we walked the deck. We were content just to hold onto each other in our new status as man and wife; we didn't talk much.

The main highway that runs the length of Vancouver Island is called The Malahat. The midway crest gives one a breathtaking view and has made the Nanaimo-to-Victoria run a favorite of tourists through the years.

About eight o'clock that night we were careening along on the very top of the Malahat when the car came to a jolting, grinding halt! We had broken an axle.

We sat there, huddled in the rapidly descending darkness, wondering what on earth we should do, when slowly nosing up over the opposite bend of the road came a huffing and puffing, smoke-spouting van. It was an enormous van, the transcontinental moving type of van and there, sitting in its cockpit, singing at the top of its lungs was a navy blue beret covering a pair of shaggy eyebrows and a dark bushy mustache!

We waved frantically—John in his natty garbardine suit, and I in my pale blue lace sheath and wide-brimmed white velvet hat!

The bushy-mustached driver smiled at us, and with a stream of French chatter, lumbered out of the van. This stocky man crawled under our car to inspect the damage, and then in another, more emphatic stream of French chatter, explained the problem. He pulled off the navy blue beret, and wiping a sweaty forehead with a red and white pocket handkerchief, his gnarled hand pointed to the cab of the truck and he said, "*Allez, allez,* we go to Duncan to fix!"

Trundling our suitcases into the sleeping compartment above the cab of the truck, John and I climbed in. There ensued one of the bumpiest, wildest rides that surely tested the "zest and enthusiasm" which Mr. Hadley had that afternoon assured our wedding guests I would put into my marriage!

Duncan was filled to the brim. The local annual fair had crowded every hotel and motel of the small town. I seemed to sit forever on our suitcases in the parking lot of the gas station while John wore out his fingers dialing through the Yellow Pages.

Finally, the owner of the gas station hobbled over. Mr. Hagerman extended his hand, and between puffs on his briar pipe, he nodded his head and said in a heavy Dutch accent, "Yeah, dot's it, dere's none. Dere all fulled up!"

Thinking for a moment, he disappeared to make a phone call; then he came out smiling.

"Momma, she says, come mitt us—we push der children togeder, and you stay mitt us!"

He explained that he would need to send away to Vancouver for another axle and that it might take a few days to fix the car. In the morning, as a wedding gift to us, he would lend us his little Volkswagen (no charge) for the week, so that our honeymoon would not be spoiled. When we returned at the end of the week, our car would be "by den, all fixed up!"

The tears welled up in my eyes and I whispered, "How good and kind of you; thank you so very much."

John just grinned his tense, nervous grin and shook Hagerman's hand, hard!

The Hagermans lived in a modest two-story white frame house a few blocks from the service station. They had a collection of six children.

Indeed, they "pushed der children all togeder," three in one bedroom and three more in another, and gave us an alcove room with a huge brass double bed and a pair of heavy beige curtains that served as a doorway. The bathroom was down the stairs, through the kitchen and to the right of the main hallway. All I had was the gossamer finery of my wedding trousseau!

Eight pairs of curious eyes followed me as I wandered through the kitchen, armed with towel and tooth brush, and eight pairs of eyes followed me back up the stairs again! The family was sitting around the kitchen table reading from a large old Bible.

The bed squeaked with every move. John and I lay there in rigid silence, trying not to giggle. On the other side of the curtains three little kids were huddled in another big brass double bed.

"Don't move," I whispered, as John reached out for me. With every turn the bed squeaked and the kids giggled. Eventually we giggled too, and it was all we could do to hold back from exploding into hilarious, rocking laughter.

"What happened to the Empress, the violins, and the crumpets?" I asked.

John replied with a whispered version of "Humoresque," whistled through his teeth.

We spent our wedding night in frustrated paralysis, afraid to even turn over, until one by one the giggling children dropped off to sleep!

SEVEN
THE CATALYST

"HAVE YOU EVER heard of Major Ian Thomas, Fay?" Sandy asked.

"No, can't say that I have."

"You'd love him! He's English—British Army—and took part in the evacuation of Dunkirk. Just after the war he had a marvelous vision about rehabilitating Nazi youth. God gave him a castle called Capernwray under most unusual circumstances. He really has a fascinating story that I think you'd enjoy. He founded an organization called 'The Torchbearers.' I have a series of tapes on the messages he gave when he was here a year ago. I'll bring them 'round if you'd like to listen to them."

"Hum-m-m, yes, of course, Sandy, I'd be delighted to."

"Confound it," I thought, "the last thing I'd like to do is sit and listen to a bunch of tapes, obviously geared to 'deepen my spiritual life.' That's the trouble with all these evangelical Christians, they constantly go about jamming Scriptures down your throat or bombarding you with books, tracts, tapes, or whatever. I believe in Christ, I love him, I'm even attending the local Bible study; what more do they expect?"

The fact of the matter was that I was rapidly slipping into a state of spiritual atrophy.

John and I had been married for two years. Taking the advice of
D.J. Watson to "connect up with some church that is really alive,"
we were attending Bethany of Sierra Madre, an interdenomina-
tional evangelical community fellowship that taught the Bible,
preached the Bible, and emphasized the necessity of an unconditional commitment to Jesus Christ as Savior and Lord.

My admiration of Sandy and basic good manners prevented me
from anything but a weak smile. She was a lovely woman whose
eyes seemed consistently to shine right out of her face. Beautifully
groomed, she was the epitome of good taste.

We were having a cup of tea at one of the church socials
regularly scheduled by our adult Sunday school class. Most of us
young women knew each other well through the mutual interest of
our children. We had coffee hours together and frequently en-
countered each other at the local supermarkets. But these evening
socials were special times when our husbands joined us and could
make some of the man-to-man contacts essential to the building
and strengthening of their faith. Generally I found them an utter
bore, and was always gratefully relieved when I discovered that we
had been included in the same company as Christians like Sandy,
Jim, Betty, Bill, and others who knew how to laugh, loud and
often, and had not become buried in dogmatic legalism or
judgmentalism. In short, I had become a bit of a spiritual snob.

"Hopefully," I thought, "she'll forget about the whole thing."

The Royal Ballet was in town and I was terribly excited about
the prospect of seeing my Vancouver friend Lynn Seymour in the
new presentation of *Romeo and Juliet*. We had spent over eighty
dollars for tickets and were going to every performance on the
repertoire in which she was dancing.

I hadn't seen her since she was fifteen and won her scholarship
to the then Sadler's Wells school in London. Letters, cards, and
pictures came regularly, but at last I'd be able to personally assess
her technique and not have to rely on the jaundiced eye of the
critics. Furthermore, we had scheduled a few dinners with Lynn
and her partner Christopher Gable while they were in town! At a
time like this, who on earth would want to listen to a series of
spiritual tapes for hours on end?

True to form, Sandy arrived on our doorstep the next morning.

She was toting a large recorder and had an armload of tapes. "Here I am," she chortled gaily. "I'm really anxious to see what you think of these! Take your time, I'm in no hurry to get them back."

After she had gone I shoved them rather disgruntledly into a closet and thought, "Well, maybe next weekend." This week was—socially—completely full.

The following Saturday, after a day of mucking about doing all our chores, I casually said to John, "I guess I'd better dig up Sandy's tapes and give them a go this evening. She's going to be wondering why I haven't called."

"Right," said John.

"I don't suppose you want to listen to them with me, do you? Hint! Hint!"

"Sure, why not? If Sandy says they're great, maybe they're great!"

He put down the copy of *Sports Illustrated*—his Bible, I called it. He knew every player in the NFL, the NHL, and the baseball majors. I needled him: "When you get to the pearly gates, I hope St. Peter asks you the batting averages of all the Dodgers, as that's about the only way you're going to get in!"

Neither of us had read the Bible completely through and I had a sneaky feeling that some ancient prophet like Haggai was going to meet us at the gates of heaven with a three-page quiz about his book!

We got comfortable on the couch and turned on the tape machine. A blazing fire threw flickering shadows across the carpet.

"Oak sure burns well," I commented as I poked up the logs.

We saved the oak for special times, as the large limbs we had trimmed from the several trees in the garden were rapidly being sacrificed to the coziness of our living room. Both John and I loved a fire—we lit one whenever the slightest nip gave a chill to our balmy California winter.

Ian Thomas' well-modulated voice started coming through. Sandy was right, he spoke well and he had a potent message.

Out of a sheer desire to win souls, to go out and get them, I was a windmill of activity until at the age of nineteen, every moment of my day was packed tight with doing things. . . .

Thus, by age nineteen, I had been reduced to a state of complete exhaustion spiritually, until I felt that there was no point in going on. . . .

Then one night in November that year, just at midnight, I got down on my knees before God, and I just wept in sheer despair. I said "O God, I know that I am saved. I love Jesus Christ. I am perfectly convinced that I am converted. With all my heart I have wanted to serve thee. I have tried to my uttermost and I am a hopeless failure!" . . . *That night things happened.*

I can honestly say that I had never once heard from the lips of men the message that came to me then . . . *but God, that night, simply focused upon me the Bible message of Christ who is our Life.* . . . *The Lord seemed to make plain to me that night, through my tears of bitterness: "You see, for seven years, with utmost sincerity, you have been trying to live for me, on my behalf, the life that I have been waiting for seven years to live through you!"*

I leaned forward and stopped the machine.

"Back it up, Honey," I said with urgency. "Did you catch what he said—about the *for* and *through?* Let's play that part again."

That was exactly what he said: "For seven years, with utmost sincerity, you have been trying to live *for* me, on my behalf, the life that I have been waiting for seven years to live *through* you."

Ian Thomas was describing me exactly. Only in my case it was practically all my life, from the sweetness of my faith under the nurturing of the sisters of the Sacred Heart Convent in Shanghai, through the trauma, disenchantment, and eventual reaffirmation of my belief while in the Japanese concentration camp, right on to my acceptance of Jesus Christ as Lord and Savior, and my baptism just a few years prior to my marriage.

I, too, had, with utmost sincerity, been trying to live *for* God, on his behalf. The frustration and resentment of it all!

Ian Thomas was saying that's not what God wanted—all he wanted was to live *his life through me!*

"Faithful is he that calleth you, who also will do it."

The One who calls you to a life of righteousness is the One, who, by your consent lives that life of righteousness through you. The One who calls you to minister to the needs of humanity is the One who, by your consent *ministers to the needs of humanity* through you! *The One who calls you to go into all the world and preach the gospel to every creature is the One who,* by your consent, *goes into all the world and preaches the gospel to every creature* through you!

This is the divine genius that saves a man from the futility of self-effort. It relieves the Christian of the burden of trying to pull himself up by his own bootstraps! If it were not for this divine provision, the call to Christ would be a source of utter frustration, presenting the sorry spectacle of a sincere idealist, constantly thwarted by his own inadequacy.

If you will but trust Christ, not only for the death he died in order to redeem you, but also for the life that he lives and waits to live through *you, the very next step you take will be a step taken in the very energy and power of God himself. You will have begun to live a life which is essentially supernatural, yet still clothed with the common humanity of your physical body, and still worked out both in the big and the little things that inevitably make up the lot of a man who, though his heart may be with Christ in heaven, still has his two feet firmly planted on the earth.*

My heart was thumping as though a catalyst had quickened its beat! "O God," I cried, "forgive me! How stupid I've been, trying to live my life *for* you. As if there was anything I could do for you, the Almighty, the Creator of the whole universe. As if there was anything I could do *for* you who spoke the worlds into being, who hung the stars in their place. Forgive me!"

The tears were rolling down my face and I was flushed with the embarrassment of my own spiritual folly and the excitement of divine potential.

The tape continued:

You will have become totally dependent *upon the life of Christ within you, and never before will you have been so independent, so emancipated from the pressure of your circumstances, so released at last from that self-distrust which has made you at one moment an arrogant, loud-mouthed braggart, and the next moment the victim of your own self-pity. . . .*

You will be restored to your true humanity—to be the human vehicle of the divine life. . . .

To be in Christ—that is redemption; but for Christ to be in you, that is sanctification!

To be in Christ—that makes you fit for heaven; but for Christ to be in you, that makes you fit for earth!

To be in Christ—that changes your destination; but for Christ to be in you, that changes your destiny!

The one makes heaven your home—the other makes this world his workshop!

John put his arms around me. Ian Thomas was still talking, but we had heard all we needed to hear, or wanted to hear at that moment. Together we slipped off the couch and onto our knees.

"Please, almighty Father," I prayed, "take over my entire being, *live your life through me.* Perform your perfect will—*whatever* you want, *however* you want, *whenever* you want, *wherever* you want, through me and in me!"

John was making his own silent commitment in response to the message. In those brief moments we gave ourselves entirely over to the authority of the indwelling presence of God Almighty in our lives.

We had a cup of tea, and then we went to bed.

Sundays took on new dimensions as we anticipated the church service in our exalted new state of being. Then it happened.

It was so trivial, I can't even remember what caused the outburst. We had what was probably the most terrible row of our marriage. We yelled and screamed at each other, something we had never done, ever, and I ended up in all my Sunday finery stretched out on the bed pounding the pillow, yelling "damn, damn," with every blow!

John stood in the doorway, sneering, "Well, if that's what turning your whole life over to God means, I'm inclined to ask for mine back!"

It was awful.

We sulked the whole morning away, and after a frosty encounter at the lunch table, began to pull together the pieces of our mutual hurts. The phone rang. It was exactly two o'clock.

"Hello?"

"Hello, is this the Angus residence?"

"Yes, it is."

"Well," a man's voice shouted, "you can all go to hell!" Then he slammed down the receiver.

I was shaking when I slowly put down our own receiver. Once more the tears came and I was reduced to a blob of emotional nothingness.

"What was all that about?" asked John.

"'You can go to hell,'" I repeated, "the voice at the other end shouted at me, 'You can all go to hell!'"

"Good night!" said John. "What's going on around here? I'm going out to saw up some more logs. My head needs clearing."

That was typically John, I thought. Work it off, sweat it out, while I'm left here to just sit and stew!

I decided to phone Sandy. I needed to tell her we had listened to her tape and I wanted to tell her about our commitment and the resulting chaos.

My story was punctuated with sniffles and the odd guttural sob as I poured it all out.

"Praise the Lord, praise the Lord," Sandy kept saying, and then as I reported the morning row and the awful phone call, she started chuckling, deep down in her throat, and then up and out in a huge gale of laughter.

"Sandy, you don't understand," I cried. "We had a terrible fight, the worst since we've been married, and then a perfect stranger phones us and tells the Angus family all to go to hell! How can you laugh?"

"Ha, ha, ha," yelled Sandy. "Fay, it's wonderful, you've both been under satanic attack, don't you see! Now that you've both turned over your whole lives to God and asked him to live his life through you, you have become a terrible threat to Satan and his demons."

At the mention of Satan and his demons I developed goose bumps. I hadn't thought about him for years. Suddenly he was there, leering at me, and a wave of nausea came over me as I remembered Ted, the demonic spirit.

"Oh, Sandy," I groaned, "how can that be? I've belonged to Jesus Christ for years."

Sandy patiently explained. "Satan is not interested in ineffective, complacent Christians. They just plod along, not doing much of anything either against him or for him. The moment you become yielded as a tool of the Holy Spirit of God, you become the archenemy of the devil, don't you see, Fay? It's warfare, spiritual warfare, that's what Paul calls it.

"Here, let me read it to you—Ephesians chapter 6—'For we wrestle not against flesh and blood, but against principalities, against powers, against the rulers of the darkness of this world, against spiritual wickedness in high places.'

"Read the book of Ephesians today, Fay, and read about how to fight Satan by putting on the armor of God."

"But, Sandy, I've been a tool of the devil." My voice trembled. "I've talked with his demons and I've been involved with the occult and fortune-telling and all those things."

There seemed to be an interminable silence at the other end of the line.

Then quietly, "OK, Fay. Settle down, you're all emotional right now. Are you going to be home later this afternoon? I want to come and see you."

What a mess. "Blast it!" I thought. My head was spinning around in confusion.

Sandy arrived late that afternoon carrying a small book, *Between Christ and Satan*, by a Dr. Kurt Koch.

"This is one of the best books on the subject," Sandy said. "I met Dr. Koch when he gave a series at our church and he explained so much that had puzzled me all my life."

I thumbed through the thin volume and started to relate my own involvement in the spirit world. I told Sandy about my dad teaching my mom and my mom teaching me; about the séances, about Ted, and finally about the mischief-makers. My stomach was churning as I paced the floor, hands nervously twisting behind my back.

"Have you ever renounced all occult involvement in your life, Fay?"

"I stopped doing it, Sandy. We got frightened when Ted wanted to take possession of me. I guess I don't exactly know what you mean by 'renounce' it." I practiced repentance and forgiveness, but just what was renunciation, and how did it fit in?

"To repent of a sin and be forgiven of a sin is one thing," Sandy explained, "but there are some sins that we have to be delivered from, and before we can really be delivered we have to first make a complete renunciation of them . . . vow never to engage in them again.

"You've probably heard people say that they've tried, but that they can't get rid of a certain sin, or sins; well, frequently it's because they're subconsciously hanging onto those sins. When they pray for forgiveness, even at that very moment, they're planning in the depths of their beings exactly how and when they're going to indulge in those sins again. It's sort of like asking for forgiveness with your psychological fingers crossed!

"Now when you come to the point of renunciation," Sandy continued, "you know without a shadow of a doubt that you are horrified and disgusted by the sin and you consciously or subconsciously don't ever want to be involved in it again. Do you understand?"

"I know one thing, Sandy, I don't want Satan controlling any part of me or mine, ever, and if that means renunciation and deliverance, then that's what I want."

"Praise the Lord," Sandy said. "Here, let's read the Word of God to scripturally cover ourselves before we go to prayer."

"The Bible says, 'For all that do these things are an abomination unto the Lord.' Ah, here it is, Deuteronomy 18: 'There shall not be found among you any one that maketh his son or his daughter to pass through the fire, or that useth divination, or an observer of the times, or an enchanter, or a witch, or a charmer, or a consulter with familiar spirits, or a wizard, or a necromancer. For all that do these things are an abomination unto the Lord'" [vv. 10-12a].

What an abomination unto the Lord I had been! A Bible-believing Christian—but an abomination unto the Lord. A spiritually atrophied, loud-mouthed, arrogant, do-it-my-own-way, at-my-own-convenience, ineffective born-again abomination unto the Lord!

Sandy took my hands in hers as we knelt on the floor. We prayed together and I made a total renunciation before God my

Father, in the presence of his witness, Sandy, of all my occult involvement. I vowed with the help of the indwelling power of his Holy Spirit never again to read tea leaves, tell fortunes, contact the spirits, or even read the currently popular zodiac columns in the newspaper. All these things had their description in the passage of Deuteronomy Sandy had read me.

Sandy bound Satan under the authority of the name of Jesus Christ. She "covered" us with the "blood of the Lord that gave us the victory in Christ." She seemed to know exactly what she was doing and to be in complete spiritual command of the situation.

In her I had an example of a spirit-controlled life. She so obviously had something I didn't, and now she was teaching me and leading me into the disciplines of committed Christianity. She was discipling me. My whole being was quickened with a yearning for more and more of God.

"I'll come over again and pray with you tomorrow," Sandy said as she pulled on her sweater. "As a matter of fact, let's get together several times this week—you really need to know what's going on in your life and you need to be completely immersed in the Scriptures. We'll study together."

I was involved in a Bible study. It met weekly and made a tremendous impact on my life. The terrible chore, which was for years my daily Bible reading, was being revitalized.

Through a series of questions relating the Scriptures to circumstances in everyday life, followed by a weekly lecture and time of sharing, I was being tantalized by all the challenging answers throughout, not only the New Testament, but the whole Bible. Not only that, but I was being tested weekly by a complete application of those same Scriptures into my own personal life. I didn't always like it.

In fact, one day I was so annoyed by the demanded commitment to holiness in the passage we were studying, that I marched into our pastor's office, thumped my Bible down on his desk, and exclaimed, "Dr. Schaper, I don't like being a Christian anymore!"

Bob Schaper didn't flinch a muscle in his face. He just pulled out a chair and said "Oh, yes, Fay? Why don't you sit down and we'll talk about it."

He took the time that day to challenge me with the Christian life—the hard places of commitment that we want to slide through and pretend just aren't there. Then he prayed with me.

Now here was Sandy getting me from the *"for* God" to the "God *through* me" stage, and then on to renunciation, deliverance, and heaven-only-knew what next she had up her spiritual sleeve!

Actually, it was only the beginning. Ian Thomas was right when he said: "That night things began to happen. . . ."

This was the difference—the cleansing, the purging of the old life, the full surrender to the will of God, and the filling of the Holy Spirit. He was the Catalyst; the Holy Spirit, Third Person of the Trinity, intervening, interceding, motivating, directing, influencing, convicting, comforting, and living the life of God Almighty through the yielded believer!

The Catalyst—the Holy Spirit—was given to be the controlling spirit in the life of the Christian, to bring every thought, every action captive into the will of the Father!

That was the meaning of D. J. Watson's prayer for me when he wrote: "I yearn for the day when my lassie gives herself entirely over to Christ . . . when she yields everything to him and he takes over ALL her thoughts, ALL her words, and ALL her actions."

"I will pray the Father, and he shall give you another Comforter, that he may *abide with you for ever*; even the Spirit of truth; whom the world cannot receive, because it seeth him not, neither knoweth him: but ye know him; for he *dwelleth with you*, and shall *be in you*" (John 14:16, 17). The presence of God, living in and through us!

John and I took a long walk. His warm hand wrapped its secure comfort around the chill of my clutching fingers. Silently, each thinking our own thoughts, we trudged along. The rhythm of my short staccato step was a counterpoint to the steady beat of his long stride. We moved like shadows through the darkness. Dogs barked as we strolled past guarded gates, and a crescent moon bounced thin rays of light through the oaks.

"Heart of oak . . ." the English seamen sang, "are our ships, heart of oak are our men. We always are ready. Steady boys, steady! We'll fight and we'll conquer again and again. . . ."

The old sea chanty kept running through my mind.

Sea chanties! I hadn't thought about them for years. Suddenly I was back in China, a little girl dressed in my tartan skirt watching the Sikh policemen, their turbans giving them the height of giants as they rode tall in the saddles of their Indian horses.

The annual tattoo and pageantry of the British Commonwealth as army and navy vied with each other over feats of skill and military maneuvers at the famous Shanghai race course.

Sea chanties! The air was filled with them, and we used to sing them for weeks after the event. "I'm going to be an admiral someday," my brother had once bragged. We had left his young body buried under a white marble slab in that foreign field. Heavens, China seemed a lifetime ago!

I was English through and through. The blood of my grandfather who was in the British Army merged with the blood of my father in the Royal Navy. The blood of my cousin and countrymen lost to the Luftwaffe churned all my instincts for battle; and now the blood of Jesus Christ, which Sandy said was the victory, had become my heritage.

I had survived the rigors of one war; now I was enlisting as a foot-soldier in another. A more terrible and deadly war, battling for the immortal destiny of men, with an "unseen enemy." I needed combat training. "Steady, soul, steady," I thought, "we'll fight and we'll conquer again and again. . . ."

EIGHT
RELEASE OF THE SPIRIT

THERE *was* more to come!

Months later Sandy arrived quite unexpectedly on my doorstep early in the morning. It was a time of rosebuds and peach blossoms in full bloom, throwing a blaze of color along the garden fence. The large leaves of the paper trees etched a tapestry against the cloudless blue California sky.

I sat under a sign in the kitchen which read: "Today is the beginning of the rest of your life."

"God," I thought, "every window of this house looks out onto a green oasis. We are wrapped in a cocoon of foliage. Truly, I could spend every day of the rest of my life in this spot of the good earth you have given to be our home!"

The silence of our rustic hideaway was broken only by the chattering of a family of gray squirrels as they bantered at the blue jay taking his morning dip in the birdbath.

My contentment was complete. Never in my wildest dreams had I expected to be so blessed and happy. The baby crawled around in her playpen on the patio; John had given me his usual bear hug, whispered "I love you, Honey," and hustled off to the office.

Sandy came directly to the point; it was her way. She was much too busy a person to pussyfoot around an issue.

"Fay, I spent much of yesterday with you on my heart, and the Lord brought me over here this morning. Have you ever experienced the baptism of the Holy Spirit?"

"Why, yes, Sandy, of course I have—remember? I was baptized in Vancouver when I accepted Jesus Christ as my Lord and Savior."

"No, that's not what I mean."

She opened her Bible to the book of Acts and read: "'But ye shall receive power, after that the Holy Ghost is come upon you: and ye shall be witnesses unto me both in Jerusalem, and in all Judea, and in Samaria, and unto the uttermost part of the earth'" [1:8]. The passage was as familiar to me as the back of my hand.

Sandy flipped over to chapter 2. "'And when the day of Pentecost was fully come, they were all with one accord in one place. And suddenly there came a sound from heaven as of a rushing mighty wind, and it filled all the house where they were sitting. And there appeared unto them cloven tongues like as of fire, and it sat upon each of them. And they were all filled with the Holy Ghost, and began to speak with other tongues, as the Spirit gave them utterance'" [vv. 1-4].

Barely taking time for a moment of eye contact, Sandy said, "Now turn to the book of First Corinthians, chapter 12 . . ." She proceeded to read the entire chapter on the gifts of the Spirit and on through the glorious love passage in chapter 13. Thank God for the Bible studies each week which were training me to find my way around the Scriptures. I no longer had to stumble through pages and constantly turn to the index.

"'He [Paul] said unto them, Have ye received the Holy Ghost since ye believed? And they said unto him, We have not so much as heard whether there be any Holy Ghost. And he said unto them, Unto what then were ye baptized? And they said, Unto John's baptism.'" Sandy was reading again from the book of Acts: "'Then said Paul, John verily baptized with the baptism of repentance, saying unto the people, that they should believe on him which should come after him, that is, on Christ Jesus. When they heard this, they were baptized in the name of the Lord Jesus.

And when Paul had laid his hands upon them, the Holy Ghost came on them; and they spake with tongues, and prophesied'" [19:2-6].

Slowly the pieces were being fit together. Sandy was talking about the gifts of the Spirit and more specifically tongues. I vaguely knew about people who spoke in tongues; we used to call them the Holy Rollers in my Vancouver days. We were convinced that they were emotionally unbalanced!

"Fay, God led me here this morning to bring you under the power and authority of the baptism of the Holy Spirit. Will you receive it?"

"I'm not quite sure I get what you mean, Sandy. I understand the Scriptures we've just read, but what exactly happens with this baptism of the Holy Spirit, and what am I expected to do?"

Sandy then proceeded to tell me of her own experience, of how she received the baptism and of how God gave her a glorious heavenly language.

"Good grief," I thought, "is Sandy one of the Holy Rollers?" She seemed much too intelligent, dignified, and stable to have become involved in that sort of thing!

"God wants all of you, Fay," Sandy continued. "He wants your body, your soul, your mind, your spirit. He wants your understanding, your intellect, and your mouth. He wants to empower you to be an effective, dynamic witness in his Kingdom. Will you receive this?"

The roots of my hair were starting to tingle and I felt very uncomfortable—definitely embarrassed. Yet I was completely assured of one thing: as much as I wanted God to have *all* of me, I wanted desperately to have *all* of God!

"Sandy, I can't say that I totally understand what this is about. But I know you, and I trust you, and God has given you to me as a spiritual big sister and teacher. If you say this is what God wants for me, *I want everything he wants in my life.*"

"Praise the Lord," I heard Sandy whisper under her breath.

"If God wants my intellect, I give it to him," I continued. "If he wants my understanding, I give it to him. And if God wants my mouth, it's about time I gave it to him also, as it sure could use cleaning up and disciplining!"

Sandy's eyes twinkled and we both chuckled at the last statement.

"OK," she said, "we're going to pray together, and I want you to tell God all the things that you've just told me. Now when I pray for you to receive the baptism of the Holy Spirit, I want you to pray and just let out any words that may come to you, even if they sound strange. This will be the anointing of tongues."

I bowed my head with apprehension.

"O God," I prayed, "thank you so much for Sandy and all the teaching you have brought me through her. Thank you, Jesus, for saving me and coming into my life as Lord. O God, you know I've turned everything over to you and asked you to *live your life through me.* I don't know anything about this baptism of the Holy Ghost, and I don't know anything about the gift of tongues, but it's all there in your Word and I don't necessarily have to understand it. I accept it on faith. Please God, you know what an intellectually proud person I am. I give you that intellect right now, to translate from my own foolishness into your wisdom. I give you my mouth to speak your words. Forgive all my offensive thoughts and words that have grieved you and take me over and pour out your thoughts and words through me. . . ."

Sandy began to pray. She thanked God for his love; she thanked Jesus Christ for being "in the midst" of us as he had promised: "Where two or three are gathered in my name, I am in the midst of them." Then she said, "Lord Jesus, I ask you to baptize Fay in the Holy Spirit."

There was dead silence.

My mind went completely blank and I didn't even know what to pray. I had never been exposed to "tongues." I had never even heard them, so I couldn't try to imitate them. I knew some Chinese and some Latin, and a smattering of French, but that would all sound so obviously faked, I just knelt there in embarrassed silence.

"Pray, Fay," Sandy whispered. "Start 'Abba Father, I love you.' Then tell God how much you love him."

"Abba Father," I stumbled, "Abba Father, I love you. . . ."
Suddenly a torrent of strange words started coming out of me. I
couldn't believe what I was hearing — odd-sounding words from
my very own mouth. And even as I was saying them I found myself
smiling and almost laughing them out! Then as suddenly as they
had started, they stopped.

"Praise the Lord," Sandy cried as she hugged me. "You've been
anointed, Fay, and you've received the gift of tongues!"

I felt very shy and awkward, but deep down I felt a strange
excitement and joy.

"How on earth can I ever explain this to John?" was my thought
of the moment. Cut-and-dried civil engineer John. Scientific,
factual, black-and-white-with-no-gray-areas John. He'd think I'd
gone nuts!

"Fay, this is the Holy Spirit praying through you, speaking
through you, being released through you. Whenever you find
these words wanting to come out, release them through the day.
This is the Holy Spirit interceding for you, strengthening you.
Here in Jude it says 'But ye beloved, building up yourselves on
your most holy faith, *praying in the Holy Ghost.* . . .'"

Sandy had picked up her Bible again.

"Now we're going to pray for interpretation for you. Scripture
says here in 1 Corinthians 14:13: 'Wherefore let him that speaketh
in an unknown tongue pray that he may interepret.'" Sandy went
back and read the whole of chapter 14 and taught me about the
ministry of the gifts of the Spirit in the church and the necessity of
testing the spirits (1 John 4:1) to be sure they are of God. We
prayed for my wisdom in handling all of this, and then she left.

I stood at the sink doing the dishes while the strange words were
released again, only this time in just a short sentence. I paused, as
Sandy had instructed me to, and prayed for interpretation. It
came, *pow*, right into my mind: "The praise of my glory shall
sweep across the earth, for I am the Lord God that dwelleth in the
hearts of my people."

That was it, short and simple, but with the power, authority,
and majesty of the King of kings. I knelt down, soapy hands and
all, awed in the presence of God.

I didn't have the guts to tell John about it: not right away, anyway. For the moment, it was a highly personal experience, just between God and me—and of course, his channel, Sandy.

Sandy was taking me to a meeting.

"It's in an old house down the hill," she said. "They meet on Thursday evenings for prayer, Bible study, and ministry of the gifts of the Spirit."

From the moment I walked in, I felt ill at ease. What seemed to be a bunch of rather odd-looking people were all singing some hymn about the blood of the Lamb. I made my rather formal greetings and sat in one of the straight-backed chairs, crossing and uncrossing my legs.

"O Lord," I thought, "I really don't belong with these people." They just didn't seem to have any "class" whatsoever.

My eyes wandered, as I socially analyzed each person. I was somewhat astounded to find a couple of doctors included in the introductions.

The Bible study started, which was all right; and then they went to a time of prayer, emphasizing the needs of anyone for healing.

I did not speak up, but for months I had been awakening with a painful stiffness in the fingers of my left hand. It was a stiffness that lasted sometimes right through the day. I presumed it to be the onset of minor arthritis.

We went to prayer, and as each person felt led, they brought out the specifics of the spoken requests and presented them to God the Father. A quiet sort of murmuring went on in the background, which I found out later was a whispering in tongues of those around the meeting. It was as though the Spirit in each one of them was praying to undergird the articulated prayer.

I really couldn't even bring myself around to joining in. I felt completely out of place and uncomfortable, although everyone had made a point of being extremely cordial to me.

Suddenly, as they were praying for someone else, I felt a warm rush of heat surge down my left arm, right from the shoulder to the tips of my fingers. It persisted, growing to quite an intense heat. I wiggled my fingers and they were completely free from pain; I had no difficulty whatsoever in manipulating them. There was no doubt at all in my mind. I was being healed.

In that moment of confirmation of my faith to the experience, God spoke dramatically to my heart.

"You, Fay, were sitting here in judgment of my people. You, Fay, were sitting here thinking that these, my beloved saints, were beneath you. The power of my Spirit is not confined; it is universal to all who believe. These are my people; you shall not pass judgment on them; they are my *beloved* people, and I have used their faith to heal YOU!"

In that very instant, I experienced a greater healing than that of my physical infirmity. I was healed of my spiritual snobbery, and I can truthfully say that from that day forward I have never looked upon another person without the exciting awareness of him or her as a unique individual, a child of the living God, created in his image, specifically designed for his glory. Neither above, nor beneath, but all one in the human race. I learned in that instant that indeed "the eye cannot say to the hand, I have no need of thee; nor again the head to the feet, I have no need of you . . ." (1 Cor.12). Rather, in every individual there is a divinely created purpose that cannot be performed by any other individual, and we are all to esteem each other more highly than ourselves!

Further, in those moments God broke my intellectual pride. I had surrendered it all to him, but I needed to do more than that. I needed a breaking through, an irrefutable, inexplicable experience of my own. I stepped into faith—the dimension beyond intellectual rationale.

In the months and years ahead I was to be confronted by so many Christians who would say, "But Fay, tongues is the *least* of all the gifts!" And I would gladly be able to reply, "Yes, and that is exactly where God had to begin with me—at the very bottom! But I praise God that the least of his gifts is superior to the greatest of man's gifts!"

Like Paul, I wanted to be "able to comprehend with all saints what is the breadth, and length, and depth, and height; and to know the love of Christ which passeth knowledge," and that I, too, "might be filled with *all* the fulness of God" (Eph. 3:18, 19). There was no limit on Paul's filling—he had everything, every gift of the Spirit, every fruit of the Spirit. As a child of God, eager to claim my *full* inheritance in the Kingdom, should I expect less? As far as I was concerned, the bottom was as good a place as any to start being filled with *"all* the fulness."

Strangely, I have known so many who have been powerfully anointed with dynamic gifts of the Spirit—evangelism, teaching, governments—who have never been quite able to come to the point of acceptance of the "least" of all these gifts. God needed to break my intellectual pride by giving me an inexplicable experience to demonstrate his supernatural authority over me before he could remold me according to his perfect will. He had to bring me down before he could lift up Christ through me! Hallelujah!

Overwhelmed by the sudden anointing of love for those particular people whom, moments before, I had mentally scathed, I cried out (interrupting someone's prayer): "I've been healed!"

There was no embarrassment. Never again would I feel the need to "put up a front." I'd been healed, and I needed to share the witness of it. More than anything else, I needed to rush home and tell John everything that had happened to me, regardless of whether he thought I was nuts or not!

I fairly bounded onto his knee in the big arm chair, knocking the book he had been reading right out of his hands.

"Well," he smiled, "what's all this?"

I've found in my marriage that a very good position, from which a wife may present anything difficult to her husband, is sitting on his knee with her arms around his neck. It's generally guaranteed to modify any adverse reaction!

I took a deep breath and began.

His direct gaze and interest never faltered. When I had told him all, right up to the current evening's healing, he took off his glasses, slowly cleaned them with his handkerchief, gently kissed me on the tip of my nose, and said, "Let's have a cup o' tea—I'm with you, Honey, all the way!"

NINE
THE CHALLENGING
COUNTERFEIT

IT WAS A CANYON where Billy Sunday and R. A. Torrey had come to rest while on their Los Angeles evangelistic crusades. Its clear, dry environment made it one of the best spots in the world to recover from T.B. Thus weekend cottages sprang up the hillsides and dug themselves into the landscape—some carefully built with rock foundations brought from the San Gabriel river bed, and others hastily thrown together. Pockets of clapboard shanties mingled with homes of solid rustic artistry, to give the canyon a Bohemian atmosphere, in contrast to the ordered world of nearby tract houses and neatly trimmed hedges.

Canyon folk were different. Fiercely independent and individual, their free-form life styles defied definition. The transient wave of renters that moved in and out with the seasons brought constantly changing moods to the rumble of life in the hills. Together with the town's famous wisteria vine, which covered over one acre of trellised arbors and was featured in Ripley's "Believe It or Not," the canyon helped put Sierra Madre on the map.

Many called it an "oasis from insanity." A spring in the desert. A refuge of quiet sanctuary away from the hustle and bustle of the big cities of the Valley of the Angels.

Coyotes howled through their domain by night and gray

squirrels, possum, racoons, and the occasional mountain lion (cougar) scurried through backyard shrubbery. A high-walled dam stood guardian against the mountain storms, run-offs, and flash floods that engineers channeled into an open cobblestoned waterway, winding down narrow streets.

Rain brought confusion to drought-ridden Southern California. When it came it was generally in a torrent. It pelted at a galloping crescendo on the rooftops and churned a deep bass tone through the storm drains. Frequently it was the prelude to mud slides that wrought havoc among hillside homes.

The canyon channel spent most of its life a dry catchall for beer cans, bottles, and other debris of the careless passerby; but in a rain it came alive and orchestrated gurgling, rushing water that drew children to its banks to toss their leaves and stick boats in the flow!

Canyon folk planted bluebell vines, ivy, and grape along its banks and fiercely defended their open channel against the progress of the engineers who sought to pave it over. Their constant quarrel with the Flood Control authorities filled the Sierra Madre Council chambers, and bumpers stickers saying "Save Our Stream" advertised their cause in and out of town.

Rustic bridges zigzagged here and there across the wash, while towering oaks wove their branches to perfectly screen canyon footpaths . . . and rows of houses, behind rows of houses, above and below more rows of houses. A veritable rabbit warren, it was a perfect place to hide or to be alone. As a place of escape, it set the scene for the subculture of the flower children and hippie movement that exploded into America in the sixties.

Sierra Madre canyon was just a short jog up the hill and around the bend from our own backyard. A country store featured a black potbellied stove, rough-hewn benches, and, in a prominent conversation corner, a claw-footed bathtub. One side had been cut down, so that, filled with cushions, it became an unusual and attractive seat.

It was a nice walk to the country store, with the baby in her buggy, especially on a bright spring day. We took it frequently, she and I, and paused for an ice cream bar or a swig of soda pop, once up the hill.

There were always people lolling around. Long-haired men with sweet-faced barefoot girls; long-haired men with thin, bedraggled, sallow-faced barefoot girls. We'd sit around and chat and I soon became a part of the fellowship that gathered around the black potbellied stove.

As the months passed and the baby grew, we ditched the buggy and toddled up the hill hand in hand. We took our rest, and then climbed higher, occasionally all the way up to the dam. Sometimes the barefoot girls and long-haired men walked up with us, taking turns carrying the toddler when she got tired.

I learned a new vocabulary. I learned that Mary had "split" or Jim was "spaced out." I learned about hash, acid, speed, and the white horse; I learned about uppers and downers and the need to crash. I learned that you had to stay "up," very high up or you'd get very sick and mean. I learned about hunger. About crashing where you could. About loving where and whom you could. About clinging together with desperate hope, and the fragility of relationships that broke as soon as one cared to split.

Occasionally some of the canyon kids walked back down the hill and home with me and I'd ask them in for a cup of tea. "Wow, far out, Fay," they'd say in wide-eyed wonder. "Is this your pad? Wow, man, you've got it made!"

"Cream and sugar?" I'd answer as I served them tea in a bone china cup and saucer.

Two years passed and I was pregnant. One of the girls in the canyon was pregnant, too. The women at the church had a shower for me and my cupboards were bulging with a layette good from infancy to age four. "A little boy," everyone said. "It's going to be a little boy since you already have a little girl."

The girl in the canyon had a layette of exactly two diapers. They had been given to her by a friend and were well worn. She was living in one room, above an old garage. Her old man was being "real nice" to her. He was a quiet guy and seemed gentle. I took her up some little shirts, blankets, and a couple of boxes of new diapers. She was "real glad."

I had my baby—sure enough, a little boy. We named him Ian, the Gaelic form of John, "the beloved." My old man brought me red roses. The girl in the canyon had her baby—a little boy. She named him Sol, after the sun. One week later her old man split on her.

We had bought a little black Nubian goat, "Daisy." We'd bottle fed her from the time she was just a few weeks old and she attached herself to our dog Freckles. Freckles, she was convinced, was her mother! The moment Freckles was out of sight, Daisy would bleat pitifully and the poor old dog would roll one eye open from her place under the dining room table and stare accusingly at me with a "How could you do this to me in my old age?" look.

"Out you go, Freckles," I'd have to say, giving her reluctant body a shove out the door. Daisy would bound joyfully over and want to play. Freckles spent months sighing her dogged resignation to the new role of motherhood.

We took more walks up the canyon hill—my baby boy in his stroller, my little girl leading her goat Daisy on a long leash, and I with a small New Testament in my pocket. Daisy made us more and more friends. The hippies loved her and would weave wreaths of ivy or flowers for her collar while we sat on the curb, or on the wall of an old stone bridge, chatting together.

I started to tell them about Jesus.

"Oh, don't give us that crap," many of them would say; "we've had that up to here," symbolically slicing their hand across their throats. But many others would listen silently.

It was their eyes that got to me. Tired old eyes peering out of fresh teenage faces; or wild, glazed eyes looking into worlds beyond. Uncomfortable eyes that kept me awake at night.

The children, the goat, and I made endless trips up and down the hill. David Wilkerson was so completely right—one does not get to know the people in a community from the steering wheel of a car or from a few selected guests in a friend's living room. You must get out onto the streets and walk with them.

I was walking with the canyon kids. As sirens screamed around the curves at night I wondered which of them was getting busted or what new calamity was developing. I was growing to love them, each one by name, as my own, these rebellious, arrogant, lost, spaced-out, lonely kids.

Sometimes John would walk up with us after dinner, and as twilight unveiled the stars, we'd tell the children: "Let's have a silent time. Don't talk. Just listen to the night sounds."

We'd hear the crickets chirping, birds settling down for the night, and the occasional hoot of an owl. The chaparral cast strong shadows against the underbrush, and here and there a century plant threw its long spike up into the gloaming. We'd pause at lookout point and see the valley lights turn on, endless against the horizon.

As darkness fell, the rock music would tune up, car doors would slam, and we'd hurry onto the shoulder of the road as wheels screeched around the bends.

The canyon awoke at night, with its children of the darkness! We'd hear babies crying and the pungent smell of marijuana clung to our clothing. "Puff it in their faces, it'll help keep them quiet," I heard the girls tell each other as they nursed their children.

Angry voices, car doors slamming, and in the background the throbbing music. I wanted to reach in and say, "You have only one life to live; don't throw it away! Don't you know Jesus loves you and God has a plan for your life?"

Instead, we dodged the screeching wheels and walked back home to put the children to bed. I prayed a lot.

By then I was a leader in the Bible study program. I had twenty-two young women in my discussion group, and it was my responsibility to phone them each week, pray for them each day, and encourage them in the faith. Our leaders' meeting was held on Mondays; it was a time rich in spiritual growth and love. The leaders started praying for our canyon kids. I began telling the people at the church of their need and the people at the church also began praying for the canyon kids.

In the summers a whole new swarm of hippies would move into the canyon, shacking up together and squeezing into every available pad. The canyon rocked with their music and its pulse quickened.

We desperately needed a house of help, a Christian ministry with doors open to any who sought it out. The canyon was a trap. Disillusioned girls had no place to go.

"If only I *could* go home," one told me pitifully, when I suggested she contact her parents. "They don't want to ever see me again. My old man would throw me out!"

"O God," I prayed, "help me please to *never ever* throw my children out, no matter what they do. Help me, please, to always keep our doors open, no matter what. More than that, to keep our hearts open—to love them 'where they're at'! Help me, please, to *always let them come home*. . . ."

I was seeing what happened to kids when they hit the streets. Heartbroken parents started to call me.

"Mrs. Angus, I hear you know the kids in Sierra Madre canyon." Then, with a trembling voice: "My daughter has run away. If we bring up a picture could you watch out for her and let us know if she's there?"

Beautiful parents, with pictures of beautiful children, mostly from beautiful homes. Drugs, alcohol, sex . . . what had snatched their children from them?

I'd carry around their little wallet-sized picture—generally a recent school snapshot taken for the yearbook, and make the rounds. One evening I went into five pads looking for a fourteen-year-old.

"Hi, you guys! Have any of you seen Janie? Here's a picture of her. Her folks are worried sick; they're willing not to contact her if she doesn't want to see them, but they need to know she's OK."

"Yeah, sure, Fay . . . and my name's Hiawatha!"

"Wassamatter, her old man beat her up?"

"Yeah, sure, if you find her tell her she can crash here!"

"Tell her folks I think she's the chick I laid last night—I didn't know her name!" Ribald laughter!

I felt like slapping him. But the prayer of Jesus on the cross snapped my memory, "Father, forgive them, for they know not what they do!"

The trouble was, most of those kids knew exactly what they were doing. Many had Christian roots. Their rebellion was deliberate and planned. I walked home with an empty heart and prayed with the parents over the phone.

"I don't think she's in our canyon," was all I could say. "I'll keep your picture in my purse and keep watching for her. God knows where she is. Will you pray with me?" Most times they would; sometimes they'd just whisper "Thank you very much."

We needed a house of refuge—desperately!

People started to help. A businessman told me one day, "Fay, I'm going out on a deal this morning to Orange County. If I pull it off, I'll tithe it to your Canyon House." He pulled it off and I had a check for $320 in my hands.

We opened a bank account. There were several Christians living in the canyon who attended a local church. They all pledged themselves to help with a ministry and work toward building a house of refuge. But where to start, who to minister?

We girded ourselves with prayer. I visited several churches and was received very sympathetically; once we got started, help would be forthcoming. But how could we get started? No one knew exactly what to do.

In the meantime, anyone who would walk the canyon streets with me, I invited along. An Episcopalian girl named Vonnie became burdened and began to share the ministry with me.

Friendships grew. Ron the beadmaker brought me a lovely "eye of god" he had woven in brilliant colors around two sticks; he did careful, beautiful work.

"Hang it in your doorway, Fay; it will keep all the evil out!"

I turned it backwards.

"I'll hang it this way, Ron," I said. "See, here you've wound the yarn around a cross—that's my eye of God, the cross of Jesus Christ, to keep the evil out!"

"Far out!" was all he could reply.

There was Susie who nearly died on our living room couch. She came tapping at our patio door at 6:30 one morning. John had just gotten up, and was reading the paper and making himself a cup of coffee. He let her in, and in the time it took him to come to the bedroom to get me up, she had gone to the kitchen sink and swallowed a handful of pills.

I found her on the couch, zonking out. She was thirty. She had been married and had two children in foster homes in another city. Her husband had left her. Promiscuity was "her thing"—that, and downers. She had had four other illegitimate children and given them out for adoption. I got to know Susie quite well.

She was under the care of a welfare psychiatrist. I personally took her to pick up her "medication" one day. She'd get her pills, then crash in her little apartment across town until they were all gone. She knew she had a time limit before she could get them refilled, and that's when we'd see her—desperate, on our doorstep. Susie needed help, much more help than the welfare prescriptions could give her. They had become part of her problem.

Then there was Frankie. Frankie had had a baby which she kept. She was sleeping with her current boyfriend one night with the baby in the same bed. During their intercourse, they had rolled over and smothered the baby. She was getting heavily involved in heroin—to forget? How could she ever forget?

Early one morning Vonnie visited Frankie, who was crumpled in a blanket in a crash pad. Her hair was a matted mess; she hadn't eaten for days. Vonnie took her home, let her bathe in scented oil, fed her, shampooed and set her hair, and got her to agree to talk to a local pastor. He came immediately and shared the love of Christ with her. She listened, with tears in her eyes, but the gnawing in her veins was too much. By five o'clock she had to go back. I drove her there, and with a choked up voice said, "Frankie, Jesus loves you. He can deliver you, he can help you. . . ."

She returned to the filth of the pad where Vonnie had found her that morning. "Thanks," she said.

We needed a house—a place of refuge, desperately!

"Don't you ever get scared?" Vonnie had asked one day.

Things were heavy in the canyon that summer. There was talk out of Arizona of bracelets of human knuckle bones, and Satan worshipers had been seen one night in our local Sierra Madre cemetery.

"Yes, very scared."

I had always considered myself chicken-hearted. Former members of the Manson clan had dispersed around the California canyons and a few of our canyon kids had been involved in a party with them over in Big Tujunga. Two of the girls had hitchhiked back to our canyon; it got too rough for them over there.

I had awakened one night in a cold sweat. A terrible fear had come over me for the safety of my family, especially the children, and I prayed, "God, what can I do? Someone has to help these kids, wicked as some of them are."

In the twinkling of an eye, as the Bible would say, the presence of the almighty God flooded the room. I had experienced the comfort and presence of Jesus Christ, my Lord and Savior; I spoke constantly with the Holy Spirit; but this was totally different. I didn't see any vision, or blinding light, actually. I saw nothing. But I felt this overwhelming presence of power, of God the Father, First Person of the Trinity. It was as though he pointed a finger directly at me, and his voice spoke to my inner self, loud and decisive, "Fear not, you have an angel with you!"

Then the presence was gone. I was trembling, but all fear was gone. God had put an angel with me. Not my guardian angel, but a defensive angel, a special angel, like the mighty Michael. I could almost see angels standing guard outside the door of our home.

"Hallelujah," I whispered, "thank you, my Father!"

I remember, too, the exact moment when he took that angel away. It was at a much later time, when my ministry in the canyon was over, and it was a most definite signal from God the Father. He was placing the work in other hands; my term in the canyon had been completed.

I was very conscious of that defensive angel, and fortified by that promise I had no fear of taking risks that probably would have left me shaking at the knees under other circumstances.

Many, many people were praying for the work by this time. One Wednesday night I was standing at the stove, making spaghetti sauce, meditating on the canyon problems, when suddenly I felt a rush of wind around me, circling me.

"Hallelujah, Jesus," I thought, "this must be more angels!"

"No, not angels," came the understanding from God the Father.

"You are being surrounded by the prayers of the faithful."

I was to find out the next morning that members at the church weekly prayer meeting had especially prayed for me that night. This was the first and only time I have ever had a physical manifestation of prayer. It solidified within me the power of prayer. Prayer was real! I knew what it felt like to actually be *surrounded*, to be protected, to be encouraged, to be strengthened by the prayers of the faithful. Fortified, I moved out in the thrust of that power.

In the middle of all this anointing and strengthening, came a devastating experience that has given title to this chapter—the challenging counterfeit.

I was on my knees one night and, as was my custom before I released the gift of tongues, I had tested the spirits (1 John 4:1), praying, "Whatsoever comes from thee, O God, my Father, I gladly receive and release; whatsoever is not of thee I claim the victorious blood of Jesus Christ and cast it out of my life forever."

I had felt especially cautious in the matter of tongues or any physical manifestation, because of my previous exposure to the occult and my psychic tendencies. Although the power of the Holy Spirit of Jesus Christ was flowing through my life, I was always aware of the satanic warfare looking over my shoulder and the very demons of hell waiting to ensnare me. For that reason, I felt a need to clothe myself continually in the armor of the Lord, and particularly in the Scriptures, which were my sure defense against any deceit or wiles of the devil.

That night, I had tested the spirit and then waited a moment before releasing the tongue, which was generally followed by an interpretation—always a source of great strength to me. Often when I sang in the spirit, or prayed for long periods in the spirit, this did not happen. But when a specific short tongue was released, it was followed by an interpretation.

This is what happened that night. I spoke out the interpretation, a short sentence which I can't remember, probably because I was so totally bowled over by the last phrase: "All praise and glory be given to Allah!"

"Allah?" The Muhammadan name of God! I nearly died. Allah? Where was Jesus Christ? It was to him that all praise and glory must be given. I crumpled even further down on my knees and cried out in anguish, "What happened, God? This is blasphemy!"

Again, the assurance of God the Father quickened me: "Fear not, this was given as a caution to you!" Then the promise came, "It will not happen to you again."

Counterfeit tongues! So the devil could use them! Of course—I remembered the whirling dervishes and other tribal babblings; this is what they must be!

The warnings that I must be cautious occurred within a week of each other. I was driving home from the store one night when I gave a ride to a hippie I knew very well. He was pretty smashed out. Suddenly he started laughing and babbling in a type of tongues. *The challenging counterfeit*. If God Almighty had not given me, personally, that experience, I would have been in total confusion. Instead, I was completely aware and unafraid.

The second incident was one that cut deeply into my spiritual life and was probably a tool that God used to redirect my total effort.

I had been in Bible study for several years. Indeed, I had even had another unusual anointing while on an annual retreat up at Arrowhead Springs in the San Bernardino mountains. It was a beautiful time of fellowship, meetings, prayer, and general sharing.

One afternoon we had set aside two hours to walk the grounds of the gorgeous retreat hotel and talk to God—either out loud, or silently; prayerfully, reading the Scriptures; or just taking time to be alone with him. A glorious silence fell, reminiscent of my childhood in the Sacred Heart Convent school when we went on an annual lenten retreat and kept the silence for three whole days.

It was a cloudy day with an Irish mist. A suggestion of rain—not actually falling, but just a refreshing wetness on the skin and moisture in the air. I had marched around various paths and bumped, grinning, into several people. Then I settled down on the high bank of a ravine behind a clump of bushes. Banks of ground fog clung to the underbrush.

God was dealing dramatically in my life. I had at that time a monthly radio broadcast over the local FM station, in which I read and shared much of my own poetry and also that of our local poets. It was a time I thoroughly enjoyed, as it boosted my ego. I was surrounded by sensitive, creative people, and submerged in the fine arts that I so dearly loved. It was certainly a time of self-glory that I reveled in, especially when I got phone calls or letters from listeners.

For several months the Holy Spirit had been telling me that the program would have to go. He had other plans for my time. But I hung on. I was praying about it on that cliff side. Arguing was actually more the word, as I continued to dialogue with myself, the voice of my conscience, and the Holy Spirit.

"It has to go, Fay, and you know that. It glorifies you, not Jesus Christ."

"Yes, but a lot of the poems I read are spiritual poems and many people have told me that they have been moved by them."

"Yes, but they can be moved more powerfully by a reading of the Scriptures. That program glorifies you; don't try and get around it!"

"Yes, I know you're right. It has to go. At the end of the year, I'll give it up."

"When, Fay?"

"At the end of the year; that way I can let the station know and I can let all the other poets know."

"When, Fay?"

"What do you mean, 'When, Fay?' You mean the end of the month? OK, I'll give it up at the end of the month; that way I can still give the station and the poets some notice."

"When, Fay?"

"What do you mean?"

"I mean right now, Fay!"

"Right now? You mean I've done my last broadcast?"

"Yes, that's exactly what I mean."

I stirred around and squirmed a little, but I knew that I was completely under conviction. I had no other choice. I had indeed done my last broadcast and the radio station and the poets could think what they liked.

"Yes, Lord, right now." I shouted it out, "I've done my last broadcast!"

I thought the sun had come out. There was a brilliance over my eyes much like the blinding summer sun that one feels while lying face up on a beach without protective sunglasses.

"Wow, the sun came out while I was praying," I thought and opened my eyes to have a look. No, the same old mist and clouds. I shut my eyes again, and again the blinding sun. I opened them—no sun, only mist and clouds. This went on for several moments until I finally comprehended—"Jesus, it's you!" I fell, head against my knees, and worshiped. When I straightened up the light was gone.

That Bible study retreat was a highlight of my spiritual walk, for it held a powerful experience that I could not, or for that matter did not *need to* explain to anyone else at the time.

Then the ruling came out, "No one who speaks in tongues may be a Bible study leader." The announcement was made at our Monday meeting.

I had to raise my hand. "I speak in tongues, so I guess I'll have to leave leadership."

My eyes were filled with tears. One other girl raised her hand. "I do, too, so I guess I'll have to leave with you, Fay."

There was a great deal of chatter among the women. We had grown to love each other, as sisters in the Lord.

"Why should they leave? They are not part of any tongues movement. Why, we didn't even know they spoke in tongues until just now!"

The Bible sudy group had been the pivotal point of my Christian walk and growth for some five years or more, two of which I spent in leadership. Leaving it was a terrible blow.

Not only had I done my last radio broadcast; now, I found, I had attended my last leaders' meeting. Suddenly I was out, by new ruling of the management.

I understood perfectly. I would definitely not have understood had I not had the experience of the challenging counterfeit—the demonic tongues.

Suddenly I understood the dangers that could come through a deceit of the spirit. Satan can twist anything to his own use.

Ever since that time, whenever anyone has come to share with me a testimony of tongues, especially if the person has just come into the gift, my immediate concern is to pray for that person's wisdom. I have seen so many gifts of the Spirit misused. Not only can Satan misuse tongues, he can misuse and destroy *all* the gifts of the Spirit. This is very clearly evidenced by the many distortions of the Scriptures in teaching ministries. Perhaps in this we've seen the greatest misuse of all, as we see cults springing up all over the world with false teachings supposedly based on the Bible, under the guise of Christianity.

There was no resentment in me, just a very deep sorrow. My spiritual serenity had been ruptured.

The local Bible study women suggested alternatives: that during my years in leadership perhaps I could negate the tongues, or just agree not to speak in them. "Give up the tongues," some of them said. "After all, it is the *least* of the gifts and your leadership is a more important gift."

One of them came to see me and told me that she had had this gift years ago but had "matured out of it." Matured out of it? I thought. How can one mature out of the gifts of the Spirit—one should be maturing *into* them!

I sought the counsel of my husband. He did not have the gift of tongues, and would have an unbiased opinion.

"Honey, how can you turn your back on anything God has given you?"

He was right. The least of God's gifts *is* superior to the greatest of man's gifts! God had shown me that long ago.

Moreover, had I not asked for "everything"—the length, the breadth, the depth, the height? Tongues was part of that everything.

I also sought the counsel of my pastor. He did not have the gift of tongues either, and so his was another unbiased opinion. We went over the Scriptures together, just standing outside the church one evening.

"It's there, Fay, a perfectly valid gift. . . . I don't think you should quench it."

I cried for three days. I did not want to leave leadership. Our teaching leader came to see me. "Why are you crying?" she asked.

"You should be glad I'm crying," I sobbed. "That's how much Bible study leadership means to me. If I wasn't crying it would show that I didn't care much about it! You should be crying with me!"

The tears dried up and we prayed together. As she left I felt a terrible sense of loneliness.

That night John held me close. "I'm with you, Honey, always, all the way!" Cradled in his arms, I thought of Jesus—"I shall never leave you nor forsake you; behold I am with you, even unto the end of the world."

I nestled in the cleft of that rock—in the arms of my husband and in the promise of my Lord—and drew strength from both.

I guess the new ruling was one of the few ways God could get me out of the comfortable spiritual slot into which I had settled in my leadership capacity in the Bible study program. He obviously had other things for me. The alternatives had been bubbling around me for the past years in the canyon, and now God was to plunge me even more directly into that ministry.

It was all part of the "Do with my life *whatever* you want, *whenever* you want, *wherever* you want, and *however* you want" I had once prayed. I renewed that commitment over and over again until I fell asleep.

TEN
THE CANYON HOUSE

THE ONLY TIME Dave Wilkerson smiled was when I told him
that I felt like Judas, "holding the bag"!

We were sitting in his office in Tustin, California.

Our canyon kids talked about Tujunga Canyon and Topanga
Canyon and about stashing drugs in the caves of Laguna Canyon. I
realized that California was dotted with canyons—catchalls for
runaways and drug abuse, and the spawning ground for many of
the subcultures that brought with them erotica, suicide, sometimes even murder, and always inevitable tragedy.

Evangelist Morris Cerullo reported from San Diego on the
more frightening fact of an increase in Satan worship. "No matter
how bizarre, how immoral, how unbelievable are the things you
hear about Satan-worship rituals—they are probably true," he
said.

He was right. We were hearing rumbles in our own area about
pagan rituals, perverted sex orgies, and cannibalism. These followed close on the heels of the Manson murders and the June 3,
1970, murder and dismemberment of a thirty-one-year-old El
Toro teacher.

Not only did we need a Christian ministry of help in *our* canyon,
we needed a web of Christian ministries linking all these canyons

to a network that would bring the saving, the delivering, and the regenerating power of Jesus Christ into devastated lives.

I felt sure that Wilkerson was the man who could best handle it. If only he could reach into our canyons the same way he was reaching into the crime-riddled streets of all the big cities. He had kids who had come through the drug scene and matured into the Christian life. They could be trained to minister the canyon house or houses. We had raised considerable funds from Christians who were interested in getting the ministry started. These could be transferred to the Teen Challenge organization, who could then take over and get things rolling.

He could . . . *they* could . . . *he* could . . . *they* could . . . I had it all nicely compartmentalized and felt an enormous excitement and relief in the prospect of transferring the whole burden over to Dave!

Sandy and our assistant pastor from Bethany, Stan Reed, agreed to come with me and one of the Christian residents of the canyon.

"The canyons of California are one of the greatest mission fields in the world today," I told David Wilkerson.

He sat leaning on his elbows on the desk, resting his chin on crossed hands. His eyes crinkled as they studied me. He punctuated our testimonies with question after question. Sometimes his replies seemed clipped and harsh, a far cry from the response I expected, after reading his book *The Cross and the Switchblade.* He was deliberately testing our spirits. He needed to receive confirmation from the Holy Spirit as to the validity of our faith and commitment to Jesus Christ.

In California cults jumped out from every crevice, each crying their own version of "Lord, Lord. . . ." Twisted and distorted interpretations of the Scriptures led to the propagation of many false doctrines. A prayerful and powerful exercise of the gift of spiritual discernment was essential. I learned a lot from our brief encounter with Wilkerson that day.

He prayed with us and said he would send up one of his assistants to take a good look around. The prospect of their direct involvement with our work seemed remote, with the increasing demands and agonizing needs of national and international Teen Challenge ministries. However, because of their experience, perhaps they could be of help in an advisory capacity.

Grateful for the time he took with us, we left with mixed feelings. The ride home was quiet and reflective. We all admired and respected David Wilkerson, but frankly, I was disappointed. I had expected a total release from my obligations and had hoped to pass along the buck to someone who, "after all," I had told the Lord, was probably "the most qualified man in the world to sort out and minister to this mess."

It had been a grim month.

A barefoot girl toting a large Jerusalem Bible had stumbled into Stan Reed's office soliciting funds for a so-called Christian House in Sierra Madre Canyon. He sent her up to see me. She came with "her man" Jeb, and we spent five hours together. It was an in-depth exposure to psychedelic religion—the visions, the delusions of LSD.

"We even got a rock band," she said. "They practice Tuesday and Thursday nights in the garage."

"Cindi?" I asked. "How'd it be if I brought up some of our Christian kids who like music and, you know, we all had a time of Bible study, fellowship, and music together?"

"OK," she said. "We'll set it up for Thursday."

The next few days my phone line was scorching!

Pastor Dick Anderson from the Congregational Church said, "Yes, I'll come, Fay."

Pastor Jim Tharp from Central Church of the Nazarene said, "Yes, I'll come, Fay."

Pastor Lynn Schubert from Christ Chapel in Altadena said, "Yes, I'll come, Fay, and I'll bring Mike for the drums, a couple of our other musicians, and a vocalist."

Twenty of us, all together, gathered in our living room early that evening, joined hands, and prayed.

"Run interference for us, O Holy Spirit," prayed Dick Anderson, "and clear the way for the truth of your gospel."

We decided to walk up the hill, singing praises to the Lord. Led by Dick, Jim, Lynn, an Episcopalian girl, and myself, with some fifteen Christian kids following, we were a startling sight. Quite a few heads popped out of cottages as we passed by.

Daylight saving time had stretched the daylight hours. The mantle of darkness had not yet fallen and twilight filtered the shadows to sepia tones. Morning glories, shut tight against the setting sun, clung to the rock walls of the wash, and the shrill cry of a night hawk turned our eyes up toward its predatory circling.

Happy, happy, happy,
Happy in the Lord . . .
Praise God we're born again,
Trusting in His word. . . .

We sang lustily, clapping our hands from time to time.

As we turned the bend up Sturtevant Drive and swung in toward number 10089, a huge dark, burly hippie with thick black hair and shaggy beard came stumbling out of the driveway. A gallon jug of wine, hooked on one finger, was slung over his shoulder.

"WOW, what's going on?" he muttered in a startled voice, fumbling with his zipper.

We stepped across the urine-soaked dirt through the gate of Cindi's house.

Three dogs nuzzled around a pile of potato peelings. On the back porch a sleeping bag was stretched out alongside several brown paper sacks stuffed with garbage. We went through the porch and into the house.

"What a welcome," I thought.

Sixteen kids were sharing the one-bedroom shack. The radio was blaring rock at top volume and the small living room was cluttered with bodies in various stages of smash. We learned later that they were shooting not only heroin but also seconal in the bathroom. Mostly, they were high on acid, alcohol, and pills.

Pastor Tharp went into the bedroom where grubby curtains

separated sections into three sleeping areas. The "old lady" of the house, a woman of about thirty, was stretched out, flushed and obviously sick. Whether she was just "wasting" through heroin, had hepatitis, or a fever with the flu, was anyone's guess. On the night stand was a worn, well-marked black Bible. Somehow it was depressing to even see it associated with this environment. Yet in it and through it, we knew, would come the sword of the Spirit with which to slay the enemy of delusion and drugs.

Ignoring the possibility of contagion, Pastor Tharp sat on the bed, took her hand in his, and began to talk quietly.

The rest of us were invited into the music area in the garage. The band was smoking pot and was missing several members. Our Christian kids filled in at the drums and with electric guitars. It was a one-car garage that had been insulated and padded to contain the sound on all sides, including the door. Dick Anderson sat down on the ground next to one of the amplifiers! As the music started he gave a visible jolt and told me later that he thought his ears would never stop ringing!

They started to play "Kumbaya." "O Lord," I prayed, "if ever you needed to come by anywhere, you surely need to come by here tonight!"

The shoulder-length hair of Mike, the Christian drummer, was swinging, and his face was oozing rivers of perspiration. I could hardly breathe! Between the close quarters and the contained sound of powerful amplification my head felt as though it would explode!

Several of us wandered out and back into the house. The group in the living room were passing the hashish pipe, sitting on the floor around the long low coffee table. As Pastor Anderson sat down with them, they passed him the pipe. A strange, inscrutable look came over his face. "No, thanks," he said, and they passed it over him.

As I tried to go through the doorway, a good-looking young fellow of about eighteen blocked my way, leaning on one outstretched arm against the frame.

"Hi," he said. "I'm Harry, and I worship the devil!"

"Oh," I replied. *"What's he ever done for you?"*

There was a significant pause; then Harry said, "I belong to Satan!"

"No, you don't," I said. *"Satan is a deceiver, a liar and a cheat. You are created in the image of God; you really belong to him!"*

The power of the Holy Spirit fell on Harry at that moment.

He held up his hand for silence from the group, switched off the blaring radio, and pointed a trembling finger at my Bible.

"Sit down," he said, "open up that there book, and read."

I opened the Bible to John, chapter three—Nicodemus and the need to be born again. No sermon, no testimony, no nothing. I simply read the Word of God, then slammed the Bible shut and sat silently.

Harry asked, "Can I have a new life?"

"Yes, Harry, you can," I replied.

He repeated, "Can I have a *new* life?"

"Yes, Harry."

It suddenly dawned on me that he wanted a new life, right then and there.

"Do you want a new life now, Harry?"

"Yeah," he replied.

"Let's go outside," I said.

My heart was thumping and I thought my lungs would burst for the want of fresh air.

That night, with the stars of heaven as our witness, we went outside and knelt in the filthy, littered yard of the house, and a young man—who just minutes before had been in satanic bondage—repented of his sins and was born into the Kingdom of heaven. Jesus Christ became his Savior and his Lord. He was indeed given new life, as promised by the Scriptures (2 Cor. 5:17: "Therefore if any man be in Christ, he is a new creature; old things are passed away; behold, all things are become new").

Satan, the liar and the cheat, was defeated by one powerful thrust of the Word of God, the sword of the Spirit for the tearing down of strongholds.

We marched around that house that night—seven times—

singing, praising God, and claiming it in the name of the Lord!

We had "landed on the beach" in our thrust into the canyon.

As promised, Rik Schultz from Dave Wilkerson's office came up and spent four hours with us, walking around. We trudged him up the back paths of the wash, side-stepping the mounds of debris that buzzed with flies. I really didn't have much to say, my heart was so heavy with the burden of the wasted young lives.

We showed him "Wormwood," the tiny stone cottage—just one room above another cut into the hillside; and the corner house with "Let the Sunshine In," painted wildly on its door. We walked around one of the compounds (clusters of houses with a center court) and looked at what I called "The Matchbox," the smallest, lowest-slung shack I had ever seen!

"You're kind of quiet, Fay," he said.

"Yeah!"

"I feel your burden," he reflected quietly.

We wound up sitting around a pot of tea in our living room.

"There is a difficult work to be done here," said Rik.

He went on to encourage us in the Spirit, praying with us, assuring us that "more powerful is he that is within you than he that is within the world."

We needed a servant of the Lord, to whom the Holy Spirit would lead us, to live in and minister to a house of refuge and help.

"I will make myself available to you whenever you care to call me," Rik said. He encouraged us to move out with the vision that God had given us. He was true to his word, and over the months and years ahead, he was a source of strength and wisdom. We were able to use the *Jesus Person Maturity Manual*, and other literature written by Dave Wilkerson, as powerful tools in our canyon.

But where and how to find such an elder or minister who would take over a canyon house?

"O Lord," I prayed, "we're wasting so much time, and lives are being shattered!"

And I was still "holding the bag"!

Cindi and Jeb had moved into a one-car garage in the stone foundation under a frame house. They had bolted the large door shut, and had cut out a "needle's eye" sliver of a doorway down one side. It was decorated with stained glass, and one had to go through sideways. A double mattress covered with an American flag lay on blocks of wood and served as their bed. There was no bathroom and no kitchen; it was simply a place to sleep. Their pad was generally crowded with people.

Pastor Tharp took some of his people visiting and ministering in the canyon and Pastor Dick Anderson did the same, using many of his parishioners who already lived in the area.

Time dragged.

We formed a board with Dick Anderson as chairman, and filed for nonprofit tax-exempt status under the name "Refuge in Jesus." Our emphasis would be on the delivering power of the love of Jesus Christ ministered through houses of refuge in the canyons of California. Jumping all denominational boundaries, our thrust had unlimited potential.

The smashed-out kids kept landing on our doorstep. Liz, with eyes wide and glazed. I had never seen her quite so hyper. She couldn't sit still but nervously fidgeted with her hands, twisting a lock of hair or biting her nails.

"Let me pray with you, Liz," I said, moving over on the couch toward her.

"O God," she moaned, "if you love me, kill me, because I don't have the guts to do it myself!"

We had middle-of-the-night calls.

"Fay, there's this girl wandering around. She has gashes on her wrists healing over from where she's slit them, and she is talking incoherently. She has no place to go!"

I had been attending some of the services at Glendale Chapel, a theater-in-the-round that was being used for meetings. And I shared the teaching and preaching of the Word of God by a group of young zealous Jesus People who had come to Christ through the ministry of Chuck Smith at Calvary Chapel. A house of fellowship had been established, called "Immanuel House," and the ministry was being enlarged and blessed by an outpouring of the Holy Spirit.

One night several young men who looked as though they could have stepped right out of our canyon gave their testimony! My heart raced. Perhaps they would be willing to come over and share a picnic and afternoon of fellowship on our hillside.

Dan Cranfill was enthused. His face was radiant with the joy of the Lord. Twinkling dark eyes and a flashing smile of brilliant white teeth jumped out of his bearded face. He had been delivered and healed from his experiences with LSD and had committed his life to serving the Lord full time.

"I'll discuss it with the elders at Immanuel House," he promised.

Two weeks later, on a Sunday afternoon, we had our first fellowship picnic and outreach in the hillside garden of one of the Christian residents in the canyon.

Dan and I walked around to meet Cindi and Jeb. We passed a hippie perched on a ladder repairing the roof of his house. I recognized him as a long-time drifter.

"Hi," I said casually, "I'd like you to meet Dan, from Immanuel House over in Glendale. It's a Christian ministry of help."

"Christian, eh?" he said. Then, taking his hammer and putting a nail against his hand, he tapped it, laughing, "Remember what we did to the first Christian—we can do it again!"

A chill went through me.

"God loves you," smiled Dan.

Our fellowship and love grew for the brothers and sisters over at Glendale Chapel. We met Karen, a modern madonna with jet black long hair and dark soulful eyes set deeply into a flawless pale complexion. She had been delivered cold turkey from mainlining heroin. No withdrawal, no cramps, no discomfort—just the peace of God and the love of Jesus Christ.

Peter, Ernie, and John were joined by many other young Jesus People from our local Pasadena area as well as from the coastline beach cities. One, Steve, stayed with us for over a month and daily trudged up the hill to sit on the stone bridge and share the Word of God and delivering power of Jesus Christ.

The Catalyst, the Holy Spirit of God, was moving in and

through each one of our lives, quickening, changing, and bringing all things together for good.

One of our own Sierra Madre boys, David Rickard, had been delivered from his bondage to drugs and committed himself to help in our canyon. He wrote out his testimony for us.

A friend of mine introduced me to reds at sixteen-and-a-half. This was to become one of my downfalls, for I became an addict to pills and a slave to the party life. The Sierra Madre Canyon supplied all the parties, drugs, and "fun" anyone could ask for. It wasn't long before I became a pusher and a supplier of drugs myself. (During this time I was still an altar boy and attended church regularly.) I thought it was all right to supply drugs for people because it made them happy. I had some of the best drugs in town and became known all throughout the area as a downer, pot, and LSD supplier. I was like a walking drugstore, but mind you, I honestly didn't feel this was wrong; after all, everyone else was doing it.

Things got out of hand and I started getting busted big. It took a lot of fancy lawyers to get me out of my trouble with the law.

Finally, fed up with life and wanting peace with God (I was twenty years old), I ran down from my home, went to my church, and started to pray. But there was no relief. I was crying out to God before the altar, to help me and to get me away from this mess, but I was too high on drugs to listen to God's most precious voice. Knowing where everything was in the church, I found the key to the kitchen. I grabbed a long, dull butcher knife, knelt down, ripped open my shirt, and plunged the knife into my stomach as hard as I could.

God tried to stop the knife; the first time I tried it bounced off my flesh. Trying harder a second time, I plunged harder; this time the knife ripped its way into the tissues and stopped halfway in my abdomen. Blood rushed out like a broken water faucet. I grasped my wound and I knew I was surely going to die.

Suddenly I heard a soft voice saying, "I will not receive you into my Presence like this!"

I hurriedly pulled the knife out of my stomach and staggered for the phone to call home; it was a call that saved my life.

I knew then, suicide was not the way to reach God. But I still did not know the way to having peace and fellowship with Jesus Christ.

A few months later, a dear friend of mine, with whom I used to take drugs, invited me to a prayer meeting. It was at that prayer meeting at St. Luke's Episcopal Church that I gave my life entirely back to Christ. I was filled with God's Holy Spirit and I fell in love with Jesus. I knew his love and his forgiveness—I had to tell the world. I committed my life to be a witness for the gospel of Christ. I became an ambassador of Jesus Christ!

Dave became active in the canyon ministry and his witness was particularly significant as this was his turf. Many of the kids with whom he had taken drugs, or to whom he had supplied drugs, were delivered and came to know Jesus Christ as their Savior and Lord.

Dan and Karen had fallen in love and were to be married.

Both had been much in prayer, individually and separately, and had come to a confirmation of their joint spirits that after a brief honeymoon, they would come and help us minister a house of refuge in Sierra Madre Canyon.

Our nonprofit, tax-exempt status had been approved by the State of California, and a house high up the main drag of the canyon was vacant and had become available to us at a reasonable rent!

All things were coming together for good.

Our board met. On our knees we gave thanks. It had come to pass! We commissioned Dan and Karen to minister to the Canyon House, and committed ourselves to the launching of the work.

A place of help to those in need, a testimony of the love of Jesus Christ, and a witness of the Word of God.

ELEVEN
PEOPLE IN MY PASTURE

KNOWLEDGE without wisdom—growth without maturity—
can be dangerous!

The Canyon House Bible studies were crammed full. Kids were
sitting on the window ledges and out on the balcony, bursting out
of what we had considered to be an adequate-sized living room.
Worse—the cesspool was constantly overflowing! The body
count ranged from fifty to seventy each week and neighbors were
complaining.

The doors of the local Episcopal Church opened to us, and we
moved the weekly meetings into its sanctuary.

Historically, Church of the Ascension was a community
landmark. Each individual rock had been hand-quarried from the
San Gabriel River bed and artistically set in place. The church's
quaint old English architecture with its adjoining lych-gate made it
a popular subject for art classes and photographers. Open arched
beams domed the interior with intricate weaving. The balance of
stone and wood kept it cool in the scorching California summer
sun and conversely offered a cozy intimacy during the winter
months.

Into the formality of its liturgical services, suddenly came the
intrusion of strumming guitars, teachers and preachers whose only

vestments were jeans and T-shirts, and kids with bare feet who preferred sitting cross-legged on the floor to kneeling in the cushioned pews! The hallelujah cry "Jesus is Lord!" echoed into the rafters, and joyful arms, raised palms up, reached for a grasp of heaven.

Bodies clutched each other and swayed in unison to "We Are One in the Spirit, We Are One in the Lord . . ." The saints watched from their stained glass windows as elders washed the feet of the new young converts.

The emptiness they had once turned over to the opiate of drugs was now filled with the presence of the living Christ, and a gut-level hunger for more and more knowledge of the Scriptures and way of the Lord demanded to be fed. Casting aside all other pursuits, these young Christians threw themselves zealously into study of the Word of God. Reading and rereading the entire Bible, morning, noon, and night, their knowledge mushroomed. They grew in the faith at a pace that put to shame many of the faithful who had warmed the pew Sunday after Sunday, yet sustained themselves on only a meager ration of Scripture.

Knowledge went untempered by the wisdom of experience, and rapid growth stretched thin without the maturity of years to support the believers through many phases. Murmurings and divisions resulted from many diverse so-called "leadings of the Spirit."

"Esteem each other more highly than yourself," preached Dan, but his brow furrowed and he paced the nights in prayer.

Into this melee came an anointed man of God with a gift of love big enough to leap through the hurt and into the heart, and a gift of teaching that had raised a generation of scripturally stable Christians.

Don Hamilton had suffered a severe bout with polio as a boy, and his legs were left paralyzed. "My mother sat by my bedside day and night, opening and shutting my eyelids, as I did not have the muscular strength to even blink," he recalled.

Don explained that his twisted feet had to be painstakingly untwisted. His strength of endurance was lined in the rugged features of his face. He was as a Paul among us.

From the moment he pulled himself up and leaned on his crutches, and his massive, well-developed arms (upon which the mobility of his body depended) extended to reach for his open Bible, he commanded attention.

For the conglomerate that was his audience, there was immediate identity—an identity of suffering, of struggle, and of victory! Don was the "I shall and I will overcome!" Don was the "through Christ, I can do all things."

To me he was "Rabbi," for I had sat under his teaching for some six or seven years and he had opened up areas of Scripture that I hadn't even known were there. His compassionate tenderness and patient travail had left the mark of his ministry deep within my own soul and spirit. Now he was called to lend his wisdom, maturity, and leadership to the canyon studies.

"O Holy Spirit of God," he'd begin, "*you* are the Teacher. Prepare hearts to receive your word and take the words spoken here this evening and use them to change lives." As a humble servant of the living Christ, he reached and touched young and old alike.

The craving for more and more teaching expanded the studies right into the Hamilton living room each week. They packed in, wall to wall, for a second Bible study. They listened to Romans, and to the Gospel of John, and to Galatians and Corinthians.

One week a tall, lanky girl dressed in blue jeans and a halter top came in late, and sat cross-legged right at Don's feet. She had a white lace heart appliqued on the crotch of her pants and the seat of her jeans was covered with a scattering of embroidered red cherries.

Don didn't blink an eye or raise a comment; he smiled at her and just went right on teaching the Word. That girl received Christ at a later meeting.

Big Mike was six-foot-seven and weighed well over 250 pounds. From time to time he was a member of the "Night Riders," and "Horsemen" bikers' clubs, and would vroom his cycle into our driveway and honk for me to come out. His black leather vest with its emblem of crossed bones and his short black boots helped him cut an imposing figure. We invited him to the Bible studies and one day he did roll up—this time not on his motorcycle but in a somewhat beat-up old car. He refused to come in but sat outside in the car, playing rock music at full volume.

"I'm going to go out there and just sit with him," I told Charlotte, Don's wife. "Maybe we can have our own little mini Bible study in the front seat!"

Mike moved over a bit as I got in. He turned down the volume so that we could talk. Suddenly he reached down and pulled out a gun from under the front seat. Pointing it directly at me, he said, "What do ya think of this?"

"I think it's a dangerous weapon to keep under your seat, and I think it's a dangerous weapon to be pointing at me!" I said shakily.

He threw his head back and exploded into a gale of laughter.

"I just wanted to see if you were chicken livered," he said.

Then, tossing the gun back under the seat, he squinted at me and said seriously, "It's absolutely necessary for me to keep that gun handy!"

He turned the volume back up and the conversation was over.

I sat there in silence listening to the blaring music with him for the next forty-five minutes. My heart was racing at the thought of what might have happened. I prayed for the compassion of the Lord to reach into and transform the life of this lonely man.

Weapons frequently turned up in our ministry as kids came to Christ from a life of violence. One day I got a huge switchblade. It was the largest I had ever seen.

"Get rid of it, Fay; it done me no good!" the owner told me.

Customarily I took these down to a local church to be handed over to the correct authorities. Under the covering of the confessional no questions were asked. But this time I was due to speak at a large missionary meeting at an Arcadia church.

"I bet the ladies have never even seen a switchblade," I thought, "much less one of this size."

I was afraid of accidentally cutting myself by fiddling with the thing, so I asked John to open it up, and I wrapped it in a towel and laid it on the front seat beside me as I drove to the luncheon.

Wouldn't you know—there ahead of me on the main street was a police blockade for inspection of cars.

"O Lord," I prayed, "help me to change lanes fast, and get me through this one!"

How on earth could I explain the presence of a huge open switchblade knife beside me on the front seat? I kept my eyes straight ahead so as not to see any wave of the officer to cross over, and I drove quickly past the barrier!

Late one night I got an emergency call to go to a house around the bend where a young man was intent on shooting his brother. The brother had homosexually molested their younger seven-year-old stepbrother, and this teenager had murder in his heart.

He sat clutching two cans of beer in his lap, while drinking a third. His eyes were wild with determination. My husband had walked up the hill with me, and while I was quietly talking, trying to draw out the teenager, the lady who had called us wrote frantic notes to John saying, "Is there any way we can get his guns?"

We never did get his guns, but the Spirit of God broke that boy that night. As I told him of the love and compassion of Jesus Christ, he agreed to pray with me.

His friends were tooting their horns in the driveway and yelling, "Aw, c'mon! Get rid of the old fool and let's go!"

I took his hand as we prayed and cast the burden of his heartbreak at the foot of the cross; he raised my hands to his cheek and held them there. The warm stream of his tears wet my fingers in an anointing more blessed than any perfume.

He promised to counsel with a local pastor and seek the best help for his family and *both* his brothers.

Once in a domestic quarrel a frightened wife brought over her husband's hunting guns. These too found their way into the church office for several weeks where they were locked up for safekeeping. Unfortunately that marriage ended in divorce. The husband's guns were returned to him—but at least the wife had removed them from the house during the conflict.

We had much the same experience with pornography. As men and women, boys and girls reconciled their lives to God they cleaned up their act. One day I had a huge plastic garbage sack of hard-core pornography brought to me for disposal. Once again I picked up the phone to Stan Reed.

"Can you get rid of it? I don't even want to open it up!"

"Sure," replied Stan. "We'll just burn it up in the huge fireplace in our den, sight unseen!"

As I drove to the church office I thought, "What if I should have an accident?" I could just visualize the local headlines: "CHRISTIAN WOMAN IN CAR CRASH—PORNOGRAPHIC MATERIALS LITTER STREET!"

New Year's Eve in Pasadena is bedlam, with people camping out and lining the route of the Rose Parade. Bikers' clubs vroom their cycles up and down Colorado Boulevard and assure a sleepless night of noise and chaos.

On New Year's Eve John and I open our home to the fifty or so people in our adult Sunday school class for a time of pot-luck refreshments, fellowship, sharing, and prayer before we all pack up and go down to the church for the midnight communion service. It's a time of laughing and crying before the Lord, and riveting our attention on the priorities of our faith.

The year the Canyon House opened, New Year's Eve was particularly significant. We were all bowed in prayer when suddenly I heard Big Mike's engine gunning in the driveway.

"Good heavens," I thought, "what does he want at this time of the night?"

I rushed out. "Sh-h-h!" I whispered with my finger to my mouth. "We're all praying. Come on in quietly, and have a bite to eat."

Big Mike lumbered his way into the living room, his heavy boots clomping on the tile of the entry hall. He stood just inside, his huge hulk dwarfing the doorway. A pair of goggles dangled from one of his fingers.

At the final "Amen" everyone looked up and there he was, a giant among us! There was a startled silence as I introduced him around. He rode down to the church with us and walked defiantly down the aisle, all the way to the front pew, where he sat and stared at Pastor Bob.

The grace and care with which our people responded to Big Mike that night touched me, and I think it touched him; between us, in the experience, there was a bridging of the gap of understanding of just what the canyon ministry was all about.

Big Mike got close to Dan and Karen through the months. He'd frequently drop by the Canyon House for chow, and under all the harsh bravura, he was kind and helpful. He was always one of the first to offer help when we needed moving or hauling or errands run. We developed a genuine affection for him, even though there were occasions when he caused my heart to skip a few beats—such as when we were talking in the driveway one day and he casually remarked, "I could karate your garage door down in one blow, y'know that?"

"Yes, I believe you could," I replied quietly.

I wondered if he had a special place where he kept his gun on his motorcycle. I could not easily forget the time he had pulled it on me in the car!

Big Mike disappeared out of our lives almost as suddenly as he had appeared. I asked one of the other bikers from the Horsemen what had happened to him.

"Big Mike? Aw, he's gone back East . . ." and then with a toss of his head and a sly wink, "to school!"

I had a strong suspicion that the "school" was none other than the penitentiary. Wherever he'd gone, the love of Jesus Christ had reached into his life and I knew he'd be carrying the little New Testament we'd given him in his back hip pocket. I could only pray that he'd read it and let the Word of God renew his spirit.

I hadn't thought about mischief-makers for years. Yet, here I was looking at them once again!

The call had come from a local downtown gift store that featured wood, leather, and earthenware products as well as unusual plants. Janie had offered to let us use a corner of her store to display some of the ceramics, plaques, and pottery that our gifted kids in the canyon had made.

"Fay," she said with urgency, "do you know anything about voodoo, or the casting of magic spells?"

"A little," I stuttered into the telephone. One hand was clutching a towel around my shoulders and my hair was sopping wet. I had just stepped out of the shower.

"I have a guy here who claims to be a Christian. He has a small vase with him. He says some warlock has put an evil spell on him through this vase. He's running scared and is in pretty bad shape. I think he's all goofed up on drugs. Can you come down?"

"Keep him talking there, Janie. I'll be as quick as I can."

Together we took the vase out back and smashed it with a hammer. Inside was a narrow glass vial sealed shut with a cork and wax. We pried it open and poured out the contents. Fingernail clippings and human hair were matted together with a dark substance that could only have been dried blood.

"Mischief-makers," I said thoughtfully. Shades of Alberni Street!

Mischief-makers were used by witches and dabblers in the occult as omens of bad luck. They were symbols of evil, devices of those who were dealing with the devil!

"We come against these under the authority of the powerful name of Jesus Christ," I said. "The victorious blood of Jesus has given us authoritative power over all evil. Let's pray together.

"Submit yourselves to God, resist the devil, and he will flee from you. Draw nigh to God and he will draw nigh to you. Father, in the authority of the powerful name of Jesus Christ, we do resist the devil and every demon of hell. Under the promise of your Scriptures we command him to flee from us. We thank you that we may walk unafraid through the victorious power of your Holy Spirit dwelling in us and through us.

"Reach into the life of this young man—clear his mind of all evil, deliver him from his dependence on drugs, restore his faculties, heal every nerve in his body, enter his life as Lord and Savior, and fill him to overflowing with your Holy Spirit."

We tossed the mischief-makers into the huge trash bin in the back alley and took the young man up to the Canyon House for ministry. He was frightened and confused and would need far more than our brief encounter in the local store—an encounter, however, which broke his bondage to the devil and planted the seeds of eternity within his life.

Drugs and the occult seemed to go together. Talismans, stone or wooden god figures, and other mischief-makers showed up frequently in our canyon ministry. Some of the most unusual were hand-crafted by a handsome young soothsayer. He told tarot cards for a living, earning as much as forty dollars daily.

He had built a gypsy-type caravan shell around his half-ton truck. It was a work of art—beautifully fretted woodwork decorated the windows and roofing and hand-painted signs of the zodiac and other symbolism formed a frieze along the base line. "I travel under the god Hermes," he told us and showed us pottery figures of his deity. He had designed and crafted a complete chess set of ceramic pieces, each one of them hollow so that hashish could be inserted. The idea was that as each piece was lost in the game, the winner would sniff or smoke the hash!

"There shall not be found among you any one that maketh his son or his daughter to pass through the fire, or that useth divination, or an observer of times, or an enchanter or a witch, or a charmer or a consulter with familiar spirits, or a wizard or a necromancer. . . . For all that do these things are an abomination unto the Lord" (Deut. 18:10-12).

The familiar words had etched themselves across my heart. The experience of my own deliverance from occult involvement had a direct witness and impact in our dealing with Satan worship and bondage in the canyon. How I praise the Lord that he is able to take negatives and turn them into positives within each of our lives!

I was driving an old 1956 Mercury sedan. It was black with a red and ivory interior and the children had pasted large pink and black ladybug stickers on the hood, trunk, and each of the doors. It was a fun car and we jokingly called it the "hippiemobile"! It ran on prayer and the grace of God.

The kids from the subculture loved it and could see and recognize me coming far down the road. They'd wave or honk their horns and it was always a matter of great confusion to them on the days I drove John's sleek silver Lincoln Continental. I'd still wave and honk and they'd peer through their windshields as though they were seeing an apparition!

The hippiemobile introduced me to Katrina. A squat, kerchiefed figure somewhere in her sixties, she trudged up and down the canyon hill dragging an old child's wagon full of sacks of

groceries. She looked as though she hadn't a friend in the world.
One day I offered her a lift.

"Sure, thank you very much," she said in a thick Slavic accent.
I took her to the store regularly after that and slowly learned her
story. Prior to moving into a small shack in the canyon she had
been living in a couple of abandoned cars.

"I do pretty nice," she said. "I fix up one old car to be a bed—it
give me dry place to sleep. The other old car I put in my things and
have pretty good place under for boxes and pots. I manage good."

It gave me great pleasure to invite her in for a cup of tea and to
serve her in my best elegant china cups—she liked nice things. We
talked of God and Jesus Christ. She knew "the Lord," and loved
him, but somehow along the way of adversity and suffering she
had become estranged from the foundations of her faith.

She started coming with me to a small Bible study that Dick
Anderson conducted for an hour each week in a private home on
Grandview Avenue. A well-marked Bible gave testimony to Katrina's commitment, the dying embers of which we started fanning
back to life.

"It's people who are important," I told my children. "Not the
rags, nor the riches, but every individual person who, whether he
acknowledges it or not, is an immortal soul. Each one is unique,
valuable, irreplaceable!"

"But what about the scruffy or weirdo ones?" they asked.

"Them too," I replied. "Perhaps more than anyone else, they
are the ones who need our care and our love. Everyone,
everywhere, is important—beloved in the eyes of God their
Creator. They will live forever, long after even the very dust of the
earth has passed away. Treat them with respect, treat them with
dignity, and treat them with love. For when you greet them, you
are greeting them in the name of the Lord."

"NAMASKAR"—the Indian greeting hangs in our entry hall. It
means "I greet the god in you." For the Christian it means "I greet
the presence of the living Christ in you, I greet the power of the
Holy Spirit living through you, I greet God the Creator, in whose
image you are made! Welcome!"

TWELVE
THE EMISSARIES
OF MELCHIZEDEK

"BATH WATER hot enough to tingle the toes, and a cup o' tea in a china cup—the prime requisites for my happiness!" I had told John on our honeymoon.

"You'll have 'em, Lovey, every day, and maybe I'll even throw in a meal or two now and then!" His eyes twinkled.

Sure enough, I had had 'em; and when everyone was off to work and school in the mornings, my special indulgence was a leisurely reading of the morning news, while slowly sipping Lipton's best blend, followed by a long soak in a tub full of piping hot water. Sierra Madre water is silky soft and . . . sheer bliss! I have reflected on moments, sorted out problems, listened to tapes, prayed prayers of thanksgiving and grown spiritually, all while half submerged. It is more than a daily ritual of cleansing, it is a daily baptism!

This morning there was time for neither the tea nor the tub, and I resented it.

Before 10 A.M., slow is my high gear. But we had to be in Topanga by 9 A.M., a good hour's drive away. Bother! Better shake a leg and get on with it.

For months I had felt a drawing of my spirit, an urging toward

Topanga and Big Tujunga canyons. I was quite ready to snap up
the opportunity when the invitation came.

"Fay, come with us to a prayer meeting! Jane and I want to go.
There will be a teaching session, and then a full ministry of the gifts
of the Spirit. It's being held in a lovely chapel at the top of Topanga
Canyon Road."

My senses quivered at the mention of Topanga Canyon Road!

"Tell you what, Margie," I replied. "I'll go with you to the
prayer meeting if you and Jane in turn will come with me up into
the canyon afterward. Don't ask me why, I don't really know why,
except that the Holy Spirit has put that canyon on my heart for
quite some time now and I've been praying that our ministry might
stretch itself out to other canyons in California. It's a long shot—I
don't know exactly where we'll be going or what we'll find, but I
feel a prodding obedience to go."

Like Paul, I found it increasingly hard to "kick against the
pricks." I felt the Lord prodding us onward, in tension with our
reluctance to move forward. Like any stubborn mule, I found that
to back up was to get rear-ended or pricked. Generally, it hurt!

Margie and Jane were part of a weekly prayer group I attended.
We knew each other well and shared those deep wells of the Spirit
that brim over whenever two or three are gathered together in his
name; the "flint rubbing against flint" to set fires in the soul, and
the "comfort ye one another."

Jacaranda trees were in full bloom and hung a brilliant purple
canopy over the car as we drove through Alegria Street. I've always
felt a heart-wrenching tug whenever I've left the boundaries of our
little town for however short or long an escapade, and my spirit
has leaped in exhilarating expectation whenever I've returned. O
blessed home that wraps me in its mountain guard!

May the Lord forgive me, I don't remember a thing about the
prayer meeting. Yes, there was some edifying teaching, no doubt,
and the ritual of supplications and hallelujahs, but my eyes were
lifted up unto the hills beyond the sanctuary. I couldn't wait to get
out, and up, and into 'em! This, coupled with a fear that we might
find nothing but tumbleweeds, churned my empty stomach and
led to a tinge of nausea.

"OK," Margie was saying as she put the station wagon into gear, "lead on and let's go! Which way, Fay?"

"I don't know," I squeaked. "Up, up toward the mountains somewhere, I guess."

I had a brilliant thought. "Let's go and ask the pastor of this church if he happens to know of any work of the Lord going on up in that canyon," I said. "Surely, being in the area, he'd have some information."

We tumbled out and paraded to the church office. The pastor was standing in the doorway of an inner office, winding up a conversation with a young couple who were obviously making wedding plans.

Chandeliers dripped in the outer office, more chandeliers dripped in the inner office, and the whole setting was one of elegant crystal, mirrors, lush carpeting, and white and gold decor.

"Do you know of any work of the Lord going on in the canyons in this area?" I shakily asked the well-groomed secretary.

"Well," she replied, "we do have a young man named Warren who has come in from time to time. He lives in a trailer up by the fire station in Box Canyon, but that's about all I know. Pastor is coming out, why don't you ask him?"

Pastor fairly exploded into the room and picked up a sheaf of papers waiting for him on the desk. After our brief introduction, he ran his fingers through his hair, then looked me over.

"Why are you dressed that way?" he asked.

I hadn't been aware that I was dressed in any unusual way. I had on a grey-blue denim house dress and wore a colorful string of Indian beads which gathered into a large circular pendant in the center. The beads apparently bothered him. They were made entirely of natural things, such as seeds, then painted, and I had thought them different and pretty when I bought them at a small boutique on the pier of Huntington Beach.

I looked at myself a bit, then smiled, ignored the question, and went on about our business.

"I wondered, Pastor," I inquired, "if you know of any work of the Lord going on in the canyons in this area?"

His nostrils flared with annoyance.

"What do you mean coming here dressed like that?" Once again, his fingers ran through his hair several times. "I don't know what's going on," he said, shaking his head with irritation. "First, there's that prayer meeting in my chapel every week, and my denomination doesn't even believe in what they're doing; then you come in here dressed like this. . . . What's going on?"

By then my nostrils were flaring with irritation.

"Pastor," I replied, "I'm sorry if my dress offends you—give me a sheet and I'll be happy to throw it around me! But . . . do you know of any work of the Lord that happens to be going on in the canyons in this area?"

By now I felt like a parrot, repeating over and over, "Do you know of any work of the Lord going on in the canyons in this area?"

My eye caught a poster of David Wilkerson. It announced an upcoming crusade.

"Pastor," I said, pointing to the postor, "if you have a concern about the validity of my Christian commitment, please put in a call to Dave Wilkerson's office—they will verify who I am." Thank God for dear Rik Schultz and his promise to help.

Margie dropped the name of her brother-in-law, a prominent Christian musician, as another reference, and the pastor settled down a bit.

In retrospect, we understood some of his reasons for concern, but at the moment he seemed a somewhat harried and flustered man.

Finally, after a long explanation of his ministry in the area, he too mentioned the name of Warren and suggested that we drive up to see him.

"Take the Topanga Canyon Road to Chatsworth, turn left, then follow on up the Box Canyon Road to the fire station."

"Thank you, Pastor, and . . . God bless you." We smiled and rushed off.

We had a name, we had a direction, we had a destination!

While Margie drove, Jane and I closed our eyes and prayed for the power of the Holy Spirit to lead us onward and the authority of the name of Jesus Christ to protect us. We claimed the hills in the name of the Lord. "The earth is the Lord's and the fullness thereof!"

I had recently heard a Sunday school teacher saying that Satan was the "Lord of this world."

"No, you're wrong!" I had thought, sitting demurely in my seat. "Satan is not the Lord of this world. Satan is the *Prince* of this world, yes, and he stalks it like a roaring lion seeking those whom he may devour. But he is not the Lord. Jesus Christ is the Lord of this world. 'The earth is the Lord's and the fullness thereof!' "

As we turned up the Box Canyon Road, we came into the country. Acres of California oaks rolled over the hills—homes were scattered, with lots of space between. It was a dramatic contrast to our Sierra Madre Canyon with its dense population of houses and people. There houses were built practically on top of each other, crawling up the hillside; while here there was still wide open range land. It was a dusty, hot day, and a dusty, hot drive.

We continued in prayer, asking the Lord for some sign of encouragement. Suddenly I saw a picture of the Last Supper peering out from one of the windows of a small house.

"Stop the car," I yelled. "Look in that window; maybe that's some house of Christian witness!"

Margie hit the brakes and we came to a screeching halt. We peered out of the car windows. There was absolutely no sign of life.

"Let's go on up to the top," said Margie wisely. "After all, we're looking for Warren and his trailer."

Another half mile or so and there was the fire station.

"Yes," they knew Warren—his trailer was parked just around the bend, "right up there . . ." the fireman pointed.

We trudged along up and found it. A small aluminum Airstream tucked into the shade of an oak tree like a silver beetle. Cautiously we knocked on the door. No answer. We knocked harder and walked around, trying to peer in the windows. No answer. Warren wasn't there.

Bang, bang, bang, I thumped my hand along the side. Had God brought us all the way there for nothing? My heart sank as we turned to go back to the car.

That's when we saw the sign! A beacon, hanging from crossbeams on the other side of the dirt road.

"ALL WHO ENTER DO SO UNDER THE AUTHORITY OF GOD."

It was beautifully carved on a rustic piece of wood and arched over a pathway of flagstone steps. Further up the road was a larger sign that looked as though it could be lit up at night.

"FOUNTAIN OF THE WORLD."

Jane and I looked at each other, mouths agape in disbelief. If ever anyone had driven up there "under the authority of God," surely it was WE. We who knew nothing about anything the sign represented; we who didn't even know where we were; we who didn't even know why we were where we were; we who had merely followed a prodding of what we believed to be the leading of the Holy Spirit of Jesus Christ!

"ENTER," the sign read, " UNDER THE AUTHORITY OF GOD."

Margie had brought along her little baby and was busy giving her a bottle in the car. She said she'd have to wait and either follow us later or sit there until our return. The car was parked close to the fire station so we felt comfortable about leaving her alone.

"O God, surely it is your authority that has brought us over here," we prayed. "Take us through, and anoint us with your Holy Spirit and with your wisdom and the power of your witness, so that Christ may be glorified in this place."

"That other sign lacks one thing," I whispered to Margie. "It should read 'JESUS CHRIST—FOUNTAIN OF THE WORLD.'"

We walked down the stone pathway—it led to a large chapel. A stone-foundation chapel rising to natural wood. A structure so perfectly blended into the grove of oak trees that one had to search to find it. It reminded me somewhat of our picturesque Church of the Ascension in Sierra Madre. We were speechless with wonder.

The door was unlocked, so we entered. It was a large room with open beamed ceiling, completely empty, save for a few cushions and bookcases. An Edgar Cayce book lay, fallen open, on the floor. A riser lifted up to a beautiful extension of the main room. A massive oak grew straight through the roof and sheltered a large rough-hewn wooden cross. To one side was a long, carved table surrounded by chairs, much like the one seen in pictures of the Last Supper. I paused to lean against the knobby bark of the California oak and absorb the eerie silence.

Then, trying to lift ourselves above the clatter of our own heels on the hardwood floors, we went through the rest of the building. A well-equipped kitchen fed into a long corridor of rooms with doors ajar, many filled with what looked like costumes hanging from racks.

Not a soul around; we were awed by our own intrusion.

The back door led out to a mountain setting of rugged boulders and hills of solid rock. From a rise to the north a grotto headed the mouth of what was now a dry stream bed, winding down through the acreage. We walked still further and clambered up a small hill. I noticed a hypodermic syringe beside some bushes.

On top of the hill was a concrete block roundhouse, its door open. We peered in and saw many bunks; obviously it was a dormitory, unique in its round shape.

Several small cottages of concrete block broke through the landscape; two of them had air-conditioners running.

"Come," I said to Jane, "someone must be living there."

We knocked; no answer. Knocked at another; no answer. Then finally a little further down the hill we knocked at yet another small cottage. There was a scuffling inside, and the door opened. A tiny lady in a long green robe smiled up at us. She had a green kerchief on her head and wisps of graying hair framed a gnome-like face. She looked like someone out of a Hans Christian Andersen story!

WISDOM, KNOWLEDGE, FAITH, and LOVE—the words were embroidered in a circular emblem around a cross, centered on the bodice of the long green robe.

"Gifts of the Spirit . . ." I whispered, pointing my finger at her chest.

"Yes," she smiled.

"I am Nekonah, Cardinal Nekonah—and who are you?"

"I am Fay," I replied, "and this is Jane. We come under the authority of God—even as your sign has said. Under the authority of God and in the name of Jesus Christ."

"Ahh," she said. "Please, come, sit down, I will call Bishop Muriel."

She brought out several folding chairs from the cottage and we waited while she scurried across to another cottage to get Bishop Muriel. The door was left open and I noticed several black and white glossy pictures and newspaper clippings pinned to the wall of her small room. They were mainly of a Christ-image figure in a long robe with long dark hair and a dark beard.

Muriel was a younger woman with bright blue eyes. She too wore the long green robe with its emblem WKFL encircled around a cross. Both were barefoot and I marveled at the way they could walk unflinching across the stony terrain.

"We come in the name of Jesus Christ to bear witness to the power of his love and to glorify his name in this place," I said somewhat shakily. They smiled and nodded for me to go on.

"I notice your sign FOUNTAIN OF THE WORLD. It needs two more words—JESUS CHRIST, FOUNTAIN OF THE WORLD."

They nodded in agreement.

"Would you mind if we made a sign adding the name of Jesus Christ to that sign?" I asked.

"No," they smiled, "we would not mind."

I told them of our commitment to Jesus Christ and of our work in Sierra Madre Canyon. They had never heard of Sierra Madre Canyon.

"What place is this?" I asked. "And what work is this?"

"We are a place of peace, with love and service to all mankind," they smiled. "Our robe is the symbol of that love and peace."

We were later to find that the robe was symbolic of a great deal more. All adults of the community wore the robe—in different colors. Green for students, blue for those qualified to administer medicine, brown for those working in the kitchen, gray for those willing to take responsibility. Their leader, whom they called "Master," wore yellow.

"Are there any others here?" I asked.

"No, not with us at this time," they replied. "There was a time when many were with us. That rock formation at the head of the stream was a fountain and running water rushed down along this bed of stones, but that was quite some time ago."

"Who is that man in the pictures on your wall—there, through the doorway?" I asked.

"Ahh," they said, "that is the Master—that is Krishna Venta. He is not with us at the present time."

Krishna Venta? Somehow the name rang a bell, but I couldn't exactly place it. Vaguely I recalled an explosion and Krishna Venta being killed in a canyon in California many years ago. Yet, they spoke of him in the present tense, as though Venta was still alive.

In spite of their smiles and warmth, I sensed a heartache and saw a hurt in their eyes. These women had suffered a great deal—a suffering that perhaps they would never get over.

As strange as they looked to us in their long green robes, we must have looked equally strange to them. Jane towering over me—her tall, blonde athletic beauty; and I, small, dark, and wearing my blue denim and unusual Indian beads, each one of us carrying a Bible. We were a sort of Mutt-and-Jeff image thrust in on them from out of nowhere!

"Do you read the Bible?" we asked.

"Oh, yes," they replied. "Everyday; we study the Bible. We also listen to many spiritual radio programs and watch the Sunday church services on television."

We were in one of the most beautiful mountain settings I had seen in the canyons of California. Twenty-two acres of craggy stone, spreading oaks, and the tumbled rocks of a dry stream bed. Squirrels scurried across our path as we walked around. Brush was growing around what appeared to be the ruins of a stone foundation. Obviously we had stumbled on the remnant of what once must have been a large community.

I thought of Margie sweltering with her baby in the car.

"Nekonah," I said, "we must get back. But we will come again."
I walked with her to the stream bed.

"These rocks are dry and colorless. With running water over
them they come alive and glow in many hues. Nekonah, they
remind me of the dry bones in Ezekiel 37. Remember? The Lord
said 'I will cause breath to enter into you and ye shall live . . . and I
will lay sinews upon you, and cover you with skin and put breath
in you, and ye shall live, and ye shall know that I am the Lord. . . .'
Thus was the prophecy for the restoration of the nation Israel.

"Nekonah, this work is now a dry bones, but almighty God has
brought us here to glorify the name of Jesus Christ. He is able to
raise up a mighty work—a stream of running water—a running
water of eternal life from which men may drink and never thirst
again—a stream that shall never dry up, in the power of that name,
and to the glory of that name! Would you be willing?"

"Yes," they both smiled enthusiastically.

We prayed together, and they gave me their card with a phone
number.

We said goodbye and walked away. Looking back at their
barefoot, robed forms standing together, I felt a strange sadness.
"God bless you," I waved, "I'll be praying for you!"

"God bless you," they waved back. "Love and peace and service
to all mankind."

The baby was sound asleep and Margie, bless her heart, was
reading her Bible.

"What's happened?" she asked excitedly. "You've been gone a
long time, something must have happened! I've been covering you
in prayer."

Jane and I were overwhelmed with the experience.

"Margie, let's go," we said, falling into the car. "There's so much
to tell we'll have to kind of unwind as we go. First we want to
pray."

"O God, great is thy faithfulness," we prayed en route home.
"You did not bring us here without reason; your purpose was
fulfilled in bringing us over—we proclaimed the name of Jesus
Christ. You have unveiled our eyes to a great need in this canyon.

Now, by the power of your Holy Spirit, give us wisdom in ministry."

Who were Nekonah and Muriel, and what was the Fountain of the World? And what was a retreat-type community of twenty-two acres doing up in the wilderness of the Box Canyon area?

Dear, sweet, gentle, loving women—the remnants of a dream? The faithful clinging tenaciously to the end of an era? We had much to find out!

Microfilm files in the Pasadena library yielded over forty pages of headlines and lead copy from the *Los Angeles Times*, *The New York Times*, *The Pasadena Star News*, and *Newsweek* magazine, among others.

"BLAST KILLS CULT LEADER, 8 OTHERS"

"BOMB RIPS KRISHNA VENTA CANYON HOME"

"HORROR OF FATAL BLAST DESCRIBED BY SUR-VIVOR"

"2 MEN BLAMED IN BOMBING OF CULT: DEATHS RISE TO 10"

"CREMATION PREDICTED SAYS LEADER'S WIFE"

"BODY WON'T BE FOUND, MOTHER RUTH BELIEVES"

"OFFICERS CHECK WRECKAGE OF BLAST-TORN MONASTERY"

"SURVIVORS PRAY FOR LOST LEADER"

"10 BOYS ESCAPE WHEN BLAST WRECKS QUARTERS"

"OUR LAST NIGHT TOGETHER . . ."

"Only one adult person escaped from the holocaust that obliterated the main monastery of the Fountain of the World sect, destroyed by a mad bomber early yesterday. She is the Bishop *Nekonah*, who before joining the cult was Neva Booth, a Denver high school teacher . . ." (*L.A. Times*, Dec. 11, 1958).

My heart skipped a beat when I read the name Nekonah! Small, sweet, gentle Nekonah—had gone through a holocaust? Anxiously and with tears trickling down my cheeks, I read the unbelievable tale.

Krishna Venta "claimed to be 'the Only Begotten Son of God' and he gave his birthplace as 'the Meta Verde Valley, close to the capital of Nepal, under Mount Everest.' He liked to explain: 'I came from the planet Neophrates approximately 240,000 years ago . . . and landed in the Euphrates Valley in Turkey which was the Garden of Eden. I have been on earth all these years'" (*Newsweek*, Dec. 22, 1958). He implied, of course, his reincarnation through many bodies over many ages!

Venta founded the Fountain of the World with one location in the twenty-two acres of Box Canyon and another in Alaska. He preached "Love in Action." He built up a colony of 163 followers. "Wisdom, Knowledge, Faith, and Love" were his symbols to live by. He and his followers became beloved in the community of Chatsworth through their many services of help. They fought forest fires, barefoot—even in Alaska they drew wonder for walking barefoot, which gave title to their nickname "the barefoot cult." They helped in all community crises over a large area and were among the first at a tragic plane crash in the mountains, helping the police with the gruesome duty of picking up the pieces of bodies and human flesh scattered throughout the woods. During the Bakersfield earthquake, Venta and his group again appeared on the scene to help. Floods, fires, earthquakes, tragedies, and all types of crises—the robed, barefoot people were there. It was their credo, "Love and peace, and service to all mankind!" Venta was considered a good and kindly leader, teaching his flock to obey the Ten Commandments and conform to the law.

Many called him "Messiah" and considered him to be a reincarnation of Christ. Eighteen years prior to the bomb blast he had predicted his "cremation in 1958." He had prophesied his persecution (or crucifixion) by cremation. At the bomb blast his wife said his body would never be found. "Don't use the word dead," she said. "He is the Christ and we do not believe in death." She claimed he had no age, since "he has been with us from the beginning." (X-ray examination of a portion of a body containing dental bridgework was stated by the coroner as conclusively belonging to Venta, and law-enforcement officials said they were "satisfied" Venta was not among the survivors of the bomb blast.) *THE PARADOX.* Krishna Venta's real name was Francis Pencovic. There was some indecision as to his place of birth, but it was either San Francisco, Pittsburgh, or Springfield, Ill. He was left an orphan when a child. Through his life he built up quite a record on charges of burglary, petty larceny, vagrancy, and later, for writing threatening letters to President Roosevelt.

He was married, divorced, then married again to "Mother Ruth"; he had six children. He assumed his Krishna Venta identity in the 1940s and this was the "turning point" in his life.

A man shrouded in mystery and intrigue, he was killed in the holocaust explosion of twenty sticks of dynamite—made up with 80 percent nitroglycerine instead of the usual 20 percent ratio. Two of his disgruntled followers, Brother Jeroham (Ralph Muller) and Brother Elzibah (Peter Kamenoff) left a tape recording charging him with immorality and corruption and their intent to kill him. They had split from the cult and tried to form their own group. They died in the blast with him, together with seven others, including a baby.

Nekonah gave an eyewitness-account interview to the *L.A. Times* in which she said ". . . Then came the explosion. It was the most horrible thing. It seemed that a tremendous force was trying to wrench my body apart. Then lumber, fragments of wood began to fall upon me. After that I don't know what happened. The next thing I remember is that I was standing outside with my arms around a couple of children. I was standing (barefoot) on some glass and my feet were bleeding. The entire building had disappeared and flames poured from the rubble like a huge torch. . . ."

The roof of the boys' dormitory next to the main building had been blown off and that building also burned to its foundations. The papers were full of graphic pictures and diagrams. Mercifully, the ten boys sleeping in the dormitory escaped injury together with another cult member, Bishop Asiah.

After the bombing Mother Ruth vowed to carry on the work of

Venta. She became president of the Seven Acting Apostles, spiritual leaders of the cult, but she stated she did not have the spiritual qualifications to assume the title of Melchizedek! Apparently Krishna Venta was also called Melchizedek. Significant, as I was later to find out.

Why had God taken me over to Box Canyon? Why had God introduced me to Nekonah and Muriel years after the terrible tragedy?

I knew it was to proclaim the truth of the gospel of Jesus Christ, and I knew it was to bring them his agape love through the witness of my friendship, but was there more?

My soul wrestled for weeks and months with the questions. I sought help and counsel from many pastors. I took several of them up to visit Nekonah and Muriel on different occasions. We witnessed together and prayed together.

I especially remember one picnic we shared. I had taken several other Christians along with me. It was a beautiful afternoon of sharing and ended with all of us holding hands, praying together. As we prayed in the name of Jesus Christ, Nekonah and Muriel kept repeating "Krishna Venta, Krishna Venta." Their souls were anchored to him.

My vision of the dry rocks of the stream bed being quickened to life by the running waters of eternal life of Jesus Christ was much before me. The openness and sweetness of these two women touched me. I prayed for wisdom and gentleness as I remembered how much they had suffered and the agonies of their experience.

Their belief in reincarnation refuted the fact that Krishna Venta was dead. They, like Mother Ruth in the newspaper interview, would not use the word dead. I tried to bring them to a realization that in their belief in the Bible, in their study of the Bible, death must be recognized as a good and valuable word. Strangely, a "healthy" word.

"For I delivered unto you first of all that which I also received, how that Christ *died* for our sins according to the scriptures; and that he was buried, and that he rose again [from the *dead*] the third day according to the scriptures: . . . But if there be no resurrection of the *dead* then is Christ not risen: And if Christ be not risen, then is our preaching vain, and your faith is also vain. . . . For if the *dead* rise not, then is not Christ raised: And if Christ be not raised, your faith is vain; ye are yet in your sins. . . . But now is Christ risen from the *dead*, and become the firstfruits of them that slept. For since by man came *death*, by man came also the resurrection of the *dead*. For as in Adam all *die*, even so in Christ shall all be made alive . . ." on and on through 1 Corinthians 15.

"Nekonah, Muriel—consider . . . in this one chapter of Scripture alone; *death, die, dead*, they're mentioned at least twenty-four times!"

Nekonah and Muriel smiled and said, "Krishna Venta is not with us at this time."

I thanked God for a Savior who said "Lo, I am with you, always, even unto the end of the world!"

I grew to love these women and invited them over to see our work in Sierra Madre Canyon and to have dinner with us. We spent a wonderful day together, touring the area, and wound up with a Chinese feed in our home.

Sweet letters of thanks came from them. "Greetings in the name of our Beloved Master, the Christ," signed, "with love, Emissaries of Melchizedek." They had taken the name as followers of the High Priesthood of Melchizedek, assumed by Venta.

"O God," I prayed, "give us workers who will be willing to go in and help these women; who will teach the Bible and conduct worship services in their chapel; who will bring the truth of the gospel of Jesus Christ and the glory of his name."

"*The canyons of California are one of the greatest mission fields in the world today*," I had told Dave Wilkerson. My spirit groaned for the Emissaries of Melchizedek!

A couple of years passed, and we had the devastating Sylmar earthquake—were they all right? Yes, they were all right.

Months extended into years—years that divert our heart's intent. Eventually I called them again.

"We'd love to see you, Fay. A group of Indians are here with us now."

"Indians? Nekonah, what are Indians doing there?"

"They've been most helpful," Nekonah reported. "They have helped us fix up many things and in return we've let them pitch their teepees and settle on a portion of the land."

What kind of Indians? I wondered, remembering the renegade tribe that squatted on Alcatraz Island in the San Francisco Bay.

I drove up that weekend. The Indians were indeed there with impressive large teepees. They had a portion of the grounds, including the round bunkhouse. I met their chief who looked at me with apprehensive dark eyes.

Helpful Indians indeed had come, and did much to restore the property for Nekonah and Muriel. Now I had the heartache not only for the Emissaries, but for a whole tribe of Indians to come to know the saving grace of Jesus Christ as well!

"Contact CHIEF," the Christian organization that works with the Indian people, someone suggested.

It was too late! The Indians came and went, like a mirage, fleeting in their strength and service. Sun-bleached stones still lay colorless, as rubble in that dry and lifeless mountain canyon stream.

"Nekonah?" I asked into the phone.

"Nekonah is not with us at this time. . . ."

"Muriel! This is Fay! Are you all right?"

"Ahh, Fay! Is this really Fay? Nekonah is not with us at this time; you know her health was not too good. Fay, I'd love to see you!"

That was but yesterday.

THIRTEEN
IMMORTAL LESSONS

PAIN—it was excruciating! I couldn't move my body at all. The fluorescent numbers on the digital clock had just spun to 5 A.M. I lay flat on my back in a cold sweat.

"John!" I cried frantically. "John, help me!"

It took more than just a few pokes to pull him out of the rhythmic breathing of deep and contented slumber. The predawn hours were always special to us.

"Faith is the bird who sings to greet the dawn while it is still dark!"

Each dawn the Indian proverb brought a reaffirmation of my own faith with the assurance of the knowledge of a God who loved me. Soon the morning light would break through the cracks in the curtains. I'd wake while it was still dark, snuggle deeper under the covers, and smugly listen for the first chirp of that early bird, knowing that it was well over an hour before I had to get up.

Stretching and squirming, I'd roll over to tuck myself around John's warm contour. Most times he'd stir enough to take the arm I'd flung over him, and gently kiss my hand. We'd both doze together, thinking our own private thoughts to tick away the minutes before the alarm went off.

It was a time of defiance of the pressures of a busy schedule and the routines of office, kids, car pools, food, football practice, and homework. It was a time to bask in the knowledge of just loving and being loved. A time for reflected memories, a time of quiet togetherness.

This Sunday morning there was no stretching, squirming, or anything other than total immobility followed by sheer panic. The darkness of the night was to eclipse the dawns of many days and weeks!

In response to my urgent cry, John sleepily propped himself up on one elbow, sending a ripple through the mattress that shocked my spine with another wave of terror!

"I can't move, not a fraction of an inch," I yelped. "Something happened to my back. Please get up . . . gently . . . and find me a pain killer."

I watched his tall, slightly hunched figure in beige pajamas stumble into the bathroom. I heard him fumbling around the medicine chest. He brought me some soma compound that I'd had prescribed a year ago for a backache. I could hardly tip my head to drink the water and swallow the pill. I couldn't raise my shoulders at all.

" I need to go to the bathroom," I groaned. We waited an hour for the soma to take effect—and it didn't! After an hour I still couldn't move.

Fortunately we'd purchased an antique flattish white porcelain bedpan from an estate sale for just such an emergency. But even that didn't bring me relief; my pain defied the necessary relaxation.

Finally John picked up the phone and dialed the doctor.

"Yes, we have some codeine in the house," I heard him say. I remembered it was left over from a surgery three years ago.

"It's probably a back spasm, a muscle spasm," he said as he fed me the pills, tilting my head with one hand. "The doctor says this should ease it enough to get you moving and into his office for X-rays."

"Get the kids off to Sunday school," I whispered, emotionally exhausted. "I'll be OK for a short while."

Within the hour, John was able to roll me over and slide me

down the edge of the bed onto my knees on the floor. Then his arms hooked under mine and he lifted me up and helped me to the bathroom and back.

When the kids returned they came rushing into the bedroom. "Zingy, zingy, hot-dog, it's a miracle," yelled Ian when he learned I'd made it to the bathroom. "I prayed in Sunday school that you'd be able to get up!"

I didn't have the heart to tell him about the codeine.

It was indeed a back spasm and I was in for six weeks of painkillers and immobility, lying flat on my back. It was a direct assault on my independence. Week by week my total helplessness and dependence on those around me was to purge me of all arrogance.

"Pain is a four-letter word," I hissed.

All work on my new book stopped. Letters of encouragement, understanding, and prayer arrived from the publishers together with a steady stream of cards of cheer. The women of the church organized dinner brigades.

"Gee whiz," said the kids, "this is better chow than you usually make!"

I learned that the compassion, sympathy, understanding, and tolerance of my family had specific limitations. It was not long before I became a nuisance and a bore.

Just as I was beginning to crawl around again and indulge myself in the intense pleasure of dipping my hands into bubbling hot water to do the dishes, or to flick a duster over the black gloss of the baby grand, remembering the fun of our many musical soirees . . . I reached up in the middle of one night to turn on the light, and slam—a wave of pain hit me and I had another spasm! In one brief moment I was right back at the beginning of another extended ordeal.

"I want to have a look at you," said the doctor. "Dose up on codeine and meet me in the emergency room."

Slowly, shakily we made our way to the hospital.

"Don't bad-mouth pain," the doctor was saying. "Pain is the body's friend—it tells us when something is wrong!"

"Bilge!" I replied. I'd known the doc for years and we frequently exchanged quips together.

I lay on my side on the emergency-room table while he examined me.

"Easy up, now," he said as he helped me sit.

Another shot of pain wrenched my back and I fainted.

"What's God trying to teach you through all this?" people were asking.

"I don't give a hoot what God's trying to teach me," I yelled in rebellion. "He doesn't have to teach me anything about pain! He taught me everything about suffering through Job. He documented it in the Bible, boils, ash heap, and all! He's proven his point."

I took out further frustration by yelling at the kids: "One thing for sure, God *is* teaching me that I haven't trained you well enough to pick up and keep this house neat!"

"Aw, lay off, Mom," shrugged Ian. "He's not teaching you that! He's just teaching you how to live in a dirtier, messier house!"

To some degree, the boy was right. I was learning that a house is to serve a family, not to enslave a family. I temporarily compromised my standards and felt better; so did the family!

They'd leave a sandwich and a glass of apple juice by my bed and everyone would go off in the morning.

"Take it easy, Mom," they'd say cheerfully.

"As though I can do anything *but* take it easy!" I snorted to myself.

I left the door unlatched and periodically the neighbors would pop in to make me a cup of tea.

The boys from the Canyon House came down to pray with me. "God bless our sister Fay. Heal her, raise her up, and restore her to your service, Lord."

In between visits I sobbed into my tissues and had visions of being an invalid for the rest of my life. Fear stalked me. The healing process was slow and labored. As I crawled around I slipped my bottle of painkiller into my pocket, afraid that I might have another spasm in the kitchen, or in the bathroom, or even out on the patio, and lie there immobile for hours until the family returned at the end of the day.

I learned the disciplines of an unanswered doorbell. The confines of a double bed. I learned that those activities we take most for granted in their simplicity are the most demanding—the joy of stacking groceries, pushing a vacuum cleaner, or just plain bending down to pick up a piece of lint.

I learned that the harsh line of pain rips across the nerves and tests the fragility of the human spirit.

I learned the weakness of my thresholds and developed a growing respect for all the interrelated functions of the human body, cell by cell and nerve end by nerve end.

I learned that the body of believers is also so interrelated that no person can make it through alone, ever! I learned that our dependence upon God our Father is directly related to and augmented by our dependence upon each other—as family, as friends, as brethren.

I learned how pain can fall like a shroud upon our commitment of faith.

FIRE! Orange tongues were leaping up the hillside, spewing curls of black smoke like grotesque shadows against the cloudless sky. I saw them breaking through the oak grove with splashes of brilliant color, moments before I heard the sirens wailing.

It had been a tranquil morning. I had taken a break away from the rattle of the typewriter to water the beds of elephant ears and bracken surrounding the pool. The lush tropical foliage in varying shades of green transported us to faraway places. Sometimes we could picture ourselves swimming in a pond in the middle of equatorial Africa, with banana trees casting their reflection in the rippling water.

We had carefully designed the pool to blend in with the rustic mountain setting. Oak Creek Canyon rock formed its rugged edge and we had momentarily contemplated a black bottom. For-tunately common sense won out, so we have clear water that reflects the blue California sky. The elephant ears had grown enormous and measured four feet long by some three feet across at their broadest point. Our missionary friends from Africa told us how they were used as umbrellas over there. Plucking a deep crimson petal from the large banana blossom, they went on to show us how it was twisted to form a funnel for feeding babies!

Now the birds of paradise standing in stately clumps at one corner of the deck matched the orange blaze flaming up the mountainside. Blue jays squawked a warning and a family of black crows cawed mockingly. I rushed for the phone.

"John, get home quickly, the mountain is on fire!"

By now the engines were coming in from all directions, their screaming harmony sending the neighborhood dogs into a frenzy of howls. Yellow city trucks, followed by green forest service trucks, were whizzing past our driveway on Canyon Road.

My first concern was Canyon House number one and Canyon House number two. Yes, the ministry had expanded and we now had two houses of refuge—the latter high up the hill, the last house at the base of the Sierra Madre Dam. Eleven men lived there, and it looked as if they would need to be evacuated.

Earthquake, fire, and flood—the hazards of the California life style. Methodically I reached for our metal box of documents, and stacked it with albums of photographs, preparing myself for a quick exit.

The war years had rearranged my values. After all, what does one take into concentration camp when one is allowed only as much as she can carry?

Mementos are irreplaceable. Even our children had been trained, in case of fire or flood, to forget the sterling silver and grab the irreplaceable picture, Grandpa's well-marked Bible, the stuffed baby toy, or the childhood treasure. And always, above everything else, remember the animals. The hamster, the two cats, and Zip the dog. The hen coop would just have to be opened and the chickens left to fend for themselves.

All our fire drills had not been drills at all—they had been the real thing. This would be the third time we'd been prepared to evacuate.

"Do we hose down the roof?"

"No, not yet. Turn off all sprinklers and leave the pressure for those in more serious danger up the hill."

Our main concern was the five-acre estate next door. One spark could set the oak groves exploding in flame and our exit out of the canyon would be blocked.

By the time John got home and I raced to pick up the children from school, police blockades had cut off all our mountain streets and it was necessary for us to stop and obtain passes to get back in.

Phone calls with offers of assistance or a place to stay broke the tense wait and we watched reports on TV about all the fires breaking out across Los Angeles County.

Borate bombers swooped across the mountain, dropping their dark loads. The fire fighters were forming their line across the trails. They looked like yellow ants in their slickers and hard hats, standing sentry with hoses ready, waiting for the fire to reach them. Strategy was interesting. They did not go in helter-skelter, but set their line and stood their ground, conceding the brush above them on the mountain.

Fire by night is more grotesquely startling than fire by day. No borate bombers to help then. The fire fighter becomes the only weapon against the orange peril. The night watch is long and no one sleeps.

At the first lick of a flame, our family goes to prayer, and friends of our family go to prayer. This is the only home that both John and I have ever owned. Our childhoods were spent in homes, but in other people's homes, rentals, or, as in the Orient, in corporation housing. We have no roots within the soil but these, and the owning of a home has brought special effort and joy into our marriage.

"Play the water on the trees," I'd say. "Forget the house! We can always rebuild the house, but we can never regrow the oaks!"

We live on the threshold of insecurity.

FLOOD. Fire in the mountains is always followed by flood in the rainy season. Rivers of mud slide down our denuded hills; rivers of mud that fill up houses and bury cars.

One year they broke through the patio door of one of the families in the church and filled the kitchen up to the counter tops. One of their children was knocked down in the flow and was buried alive for a frantic minute and a half while her parents clawed their way through the slime to dig her out. What if they hadn't seen where she had been standing? What if she had been alone in the room!

Years afterward, raindrops on the roof sent chills of panic through that mother's heart!

On my kitchen window ledge, above the sink, where I spend so many happy moments puttering around, is a rock. A special rock—a flood-tide rock, full of tunnels carved by snails and worms, with a few bits of shell left here and there where some sea creature made its home centuries ago.

John had that rock analyzed by one of his geologists. It has survived not only generations, but entire civilizations. I contemplate it daily. It teaches me: of Jehovah who asked of Job, "Where wast thou when I laid the foundations of the earth?" (Job 38:4). That rock, in all its silent, stoic gray, articulates, "Where were you, Fay, when I was formed? Where will you be a generation from now?"

With a bent head and hushed heart I answer.

"When you were formed, I was in the bosom of my Father—a generation from now, I will be returned to the bosom of my Father, while you, O rock, will remain a rock, gathering the mud of the flood tides and drying out under the scorching sun of the ages!"

It slows me down. When cluttered about with schedules and chores, I stop. One hundred years from now who will know or care that I dusted the piano, or scrubbed the kitchen floor, or laughed happy laughs with friends, or cried salty tears alone?

Then I look to another Rock. He's called the Rock of Ages; he will know and care.

He laid the foundations of the earth and heard the morning stars sing together. He shut up the sea and made the clouds its garments. He knows where light dwells and the place of darkness. He gendered the hoary frost of heaven and made the treasures of the snow (Job 38). And from the dust of the earth, he formed me, and made me. In his own image, he formed me and made me!

Our length of days is measured by the immortal lessons learned and lived through our commitment in faith—a commitment that will be cradled in the eternity of our destiny forever and evermore. OBEDIENCE. It's a one-word summary of commitment. You either obey or you don't. For those who try to live in the nebulous in-between, it means years of ineffectual treading water and spinning in the widening circles of compromise and doubt.

The obedience of my commitment to Jesus Christ is one called out and away from convenience. The calls to action in and through my life startled me, until my wincing hesitation was finally strengthened to the point of total, confident trust.

For instance, the morning the phone rang and the voice at the other end said, "Mrs. Angus? Vice and Narcotics calling . . . I think it's about time we had a little chat."

I was in the middle of coordinating a task force against hard-core pornography. After attending a Church Women United forum on pornography and learning that there is indeed much that can be done by the "moral community" to combat this blight, I was faced with the decision of response—the awesome responsibility of knowledge. What do we do with it? File it in the archives of our heart, or fall to our knees and say, "What would thou have me to do, Lord?"

Hard-core pornography is not the girlie magazine, or the odd R-rated movie; hard-core pornography is complete and utter depravity. The bestiality, the sodomy, the violence of the "snuff" film (murder by dismemberment and sex)—is the vilest degeneracy ever exhibited by the human race.

"Oh, God," I groaned, "while we sit in our pews Sunday by Sunday, just a few hundred yards away up and down the street, five porno houses are showing and selling this abominatiion!"

"And what are *you* going to do about it, Fay?" The conviction of conscience.

Little did I know that I was about to be thrust into the very groin of our society.

We stand on the threshold of moral suicide. With headlines shrieking VD as pandemic (totally out of control), over one million teenage pregnancies annually in the United States, 30,000 children used in child pornography in the greater Los Angeles area alone, the promotion of "intrafamily" sex (incest) and deviate, disoriented sexual activity on the increase, we are in a state of moral crisis.

I remembered a TV interview with the famed historian Ariel Durant. She was asked if in all her research and experience there was *a woman* who stood out uniquely as having contributed the most to civilization.

Without a moment's hesitation, she answered, "Not *a woman*, but *women!* The women of the thirteenth century!" She went on to explain how at that brutal time of history those women preserved education, preserved culture, preserved their religious convictions, and preserved morality.

"O God," I prayed, "when the history of this generation is written, let me be counted among the men and women who will commit themselves to the same preservations within this permissive and degenerating society!"

Obedience! This call to action in my life to raise up a standard of decency was to thrust me into the sordid world of pornography, public debates with homosexuals and lesbians, an NBC interview and CBS editorial rebuttal, and direct contact with many of our legislators.

"O God," I prayed, "I am not afraid of failing; I am only afraid of never trying!" I stepped out and set my mark for decency.

Our pledge of allegiance to the gospel of Jesus Christ, the immortal lessons learned through our uncompromising obedience to the leading of his Holy Spirit, and our everlasting servitude in the Kingdom of God—these reflect the "*Whatever, however, whenever, wherever.* . . .Thy will be done, in earth, as it is in heaven!"